# brilliant
## interview

# Books that make you better

Books that make you better. That make you *be* better, *do* better, *feel* better. Whether you want to upgrade your personal skills or change your job, whether you want to improve your managerial style, become a more powerful communicator, or be stimulated and inspired as you work.

*Prentice Hall Business* is leading the field with a new breed of skills, careers and development books. Books that are a cut above the mainstream – in topic, content and delivery – with an edge and verve that will make you better, with less effort.

Books that are as sharp and smart as you are.

*Prentice Hall Business.*
We work harder – so you don't have to.

For more details on products, and to contact us, visit
**www.pearsoned.co.uk**

# brilliant interview

What employers want to hear
and how to say it

second edition

## Ros Jay

PEARSON
Prentice Hall
BUSINESS

Harlow, England • London • New York • Boston • San Francisco • Toronto
Sydney • Tokyo • Singapore • Hong Kong • Seoul • Taipei • New Delhi
Cape Town • Madrid • Mexico City • Amsterdam • Munich • Paris • Milan

PEARSON EDUCATION LIMITED

Edinburgh Gate
Harlow CM20 2JE
Tel: +44 (0)1279 623623
Fax: +44 (0)1279 431059

Website: www.pearsoned.co.uk

First published 2002
**Second edition published in Great Britain 2005**

© Ros Jay 2002, 2005

The right of Ros Jay to be identified as author of this work has been asserted by her in accordance with the Copyright, Designs and Patents Act 1988.

ISBN 0 273 70356 0

*British Library Cataloguing-in-Publication Data*
A catalogue record for this book is available from the British Library.

*Library of Congress Cataloging-in-Publication Data*

Jay, Ros.
    Brilliant interview : what employers want to hear you say and how to say it / Ros Jay.—
2nd ed.
       p. cm.
    ISBN 0-273-70356-0 (pbk.)
    1. Employment interviewing. 2. Job hunting. I.Title.

HF5549.5.I6J39 2005
650.14′4—dc22                                                    2005043140

10 9 8 7 6 5 4 3 2 1
09 08 07 06 05

Designed by Claire Brodmann Book Designs, Lichfield, Staffs.
Typeset Latin 725 and HelveticaNeue by 70
Printed and bound in Great Britain by Bell & Bain Ltd, Glasgow

*The Publisher's policy is to use paper manufactured from sustainable forests.*

# Contents

# Acknowledgements

I would like to thank the many people and organizations who have helped with this book, especially:

- ASE Solutions (*www.ase-solutions.co.uk*)
- Career World
- Chartered Institute of Marketing
- Ann Pinn, MD, Delta Consultants (*www.delta-consultants.com*)
- Fish4.co.uk
- Hobsons (*www.hobsons.co.uk*)
- Penny Glazzard, Marketing Executive, Hill McGlynn (*www.hillmcglyn.com*)
- Jason Silk, Hill McGlynn
- The Institute for Employment Studies
- Oneclickhr.com
- Phil Boyle, MD, Ramsey Hall Limited (*www.ramseyhall.com*)

I would also like to acknowledge the assistance given by SHL Group plc in allowing certain parts of their example questions to be reproduced here. Further details of their materials can be obtained from the SHL website at *shlgroup.com* or by contacting the client support centre on 0870 070 7000.

In some instances we may have been unable to trace the owners of copyright material, and we would appreciate any information that would enable us to do so.

# Introduction

A job interview is a big deal. Whether or not you get the job you're going for can influence your career hugely and affect your whole life. I'm not trying to scare you here, but the fact is that how you handle the interview is important. Very important.

The interviewer isn't going to bother to call anyone for interview unless they have something promising to offer. So the other candidates are all going to be good. Which means that you'll need to be even better than them to win the job.

But it's OK. You can do it. You just need to know exactly what the interviewer is looking for. That's what *Brilliant Interview* is all about. You'll find all you need to know about presenting yourself as the best candidate, with plenty of tips and advice from the experts to tell you what they want to see and what impresses them the most.

Interviews are nerve-racking and we sometimes make mistakes, or simply don't make the most of ourselves. So arm yourself with the advantage of knowing what your interviewer is looking for and being in a position to supply it. Learn to show yourself in the best possible light and maximize your chances of getting the job.

The challenge of winning the job begins before you even turn up for the interview, and continues through your meeting with the interviewer and beyond. When you're offered the job, you still need to decide whether to take it and – if you do – how to get the best deal you can. Before, during and after the interview, there are plenty of steps you can take to set yourself above and apart from the competition.

The very fact that you have an interview (perhaps several) lined up is a great start. Every interview you get is a feather in your cap. It will almost always put you in the minority of applicants, and means that the interviewer sees you as someone who, on paper, is capable of doing the job they are advertising. So you're already well on the way to winning the job. And once you've read this book, you'll have no trouble staying the distance.

So listen to the experts, find out what they want, and before too long you should find yourself in the enviable position of deciding whether to say yes or no to a job offer.

# part one

# before
# the
## interview

# 1 What to expect

Congratulations! You've got an interview. You must have impressed the interviewer already with your CV and your application form to get this far. They're not likely to be interviewing every candidate, so clearly they've already seen something in your application that stands out from the crowd.

Of course, from your point of view, that probably seemed like the easy bit compared with the interview to come. But don't worry. Once you know what you're doing – and you will by the time you've read this book – winning the job you're going for will be easy too. Your preparation starts here. And the first thing that will help you give a brilliant interview is knowing just what to expect. The fewer surprises the better. So what's going to happen at your interview?

## Put yourself in the interviewer's shoes

You need to know what the interviewer is up to – why are they conducting these interviews? They will have started out with a pile of applications which they have sifted through and slimmed down to the people whom they are inviting for interview – including you.

The interviewer isn't going to invite anyone whom they don't reckon can do the job, so the list of interviewees will be made up entirely of people who, in the interviewer's opinion, should be capable of doing the job. Once again, you should be encouraged by this. You wouldn't be on the list unless the interviewer thought – on the basis of your application and CV – that you could do the job they are advertising.

But the interviewer has a problem. They are spoilt for choice. They have a list of maybe half a dozen or a dozen applicants, all of whom they think ought to be able to do the job. So who do they offer it to? They need more information before they can decide, and that's what the interviews are for.

## Did you know?

Not all countries use interviews as frequently as UK companies do. In other countries, organizations use a range of selection methods which don't necessarily include interviews at all (although they often do). But in the UK, 99 per cent of organizations use selection interviews to recruit new people. And 50 per cent of them use no other method alongside interviews – that's not psychometric tests, assessment centres and so on. This means that your skills as an interviewee are vital in winning just about any job you apply for.

Source: *www.oneclickhr.com*, HR Information – Selection Interviews

The interviewer has to decide which of the candidates is going to be most suited to the job. They aren't trying to measure you against each other, but against the standards for the job itself. One of you may be far more experienced than another, but experience may not be the most important thing. Perhaps fitting in with the team will matter more, or skill using a particular piece of software.

Even so, it's going to be a hard choice. All the candidates will have strong and weak points, and the interviewer will have to balance these against each other. Do they want someone who has long experience, or would they rather go for someone with shorter but more relevant experience? What if the person with the least appropriate qualifications looks as if they'll fit in best with the company culture? Should they opt for the person who looks reliable and solid, or the more creative candidate who seems less reliable?

It's tough being an interviewer. And it's tough for you too, because you know less about what they're looking for than they do. However, even if you don't know what their priorities are, you know broadly what they're after. And if you know where your strengths and weaknesses are, you can prepare to promote your strong points and find ways of making your weak spots look less like weaknesses. We'll be looking at techniques for doing this later on but, in the meantime, you can start the process by identifying your plus and minus points using this exercise.

## Assess yourself for the job

Mark yourself, on a scale of one to ten, on the following key areas your interviewer will be looking closely at. You need to assess yourself for the particular job in question so, if you have more than one interview coming up, go through the exercise for each one.

You need to compare yourself with what the interviewer will be looking for in each case, much of which will be clear from the recruitment ad, and from the job description which you should be able to get a copy of if you ask. Mark yourself out of ten for each area so you can see where you have the most work to do. When it comes to personality, you may want to ask a good friend or colleague for an honest opinion.

| Key area | 1–10 |
| --- | --- |
| Skills | |
| Direct experience of relevant tasks | |
| Qualifications | |
| Background | |
| Personality (as it comes across at interview) | |

# The basic materials

Well, at least your poor old interviewer doesn't have to make their choice blind. Even before they meet the candidates, they have no fewer than four documents to help them towards their decision. These fall into two categories: documents that help them define the job, and documents that help them assess the candidates. The documents which help them define the job are:

- the job description, which tells them the overall objective of the job, and the key responsibilities within it
- the employee specification, which describes for them what skills and attributes the successful applicant will need to have.

You should have a copy of the job description yourself, which is how you have assessed your ability to do the job. After all, your self-assessment is really a matter of looking at what you've got to offer against what they want. However, very few employers will show applicants the employee specification. It's a bit like showing someone their exam paper in advance – they'll prepare the answers they know you want to hear.

But you do have the other two pieces of paperwork, the ones which tell the interviewer what sort of person you are:

- your CV
- your application form.

Your interviewer is trying to match up this pair of documents with the first pair – in other words they're trying to find the applicant who most closely matches the job requirements. Your job is to demonstrate that you are the one.

## Selection savvy

Make a copy of your application form as well as your CV before you send it off. That way, you'll have a record of exactly what you've told the interviewer, and you can make sure you're ready with answers to all the questions they may ask arising from your application.

The interviewer – if they know anything at all about interviewing – will have two lists of questions to ask you:

- They will have a list of questions to ask all the candidates, which are questions about the job which they draw up using the first two documents – the job description and the employee specification. Unless they ask you all the same questions, it's going to be almost impossible to assess which one of you best suits the job.

- Then they will have a list of questions specifically for you, which they have formulated by looking through your application form and your CV. These might be questions about your own experience, skills, qualifications or circumstances, and about your career, your interests and your working style.

## The format

Virtually every interview follows the same basic format. If you're not used to this, it helps to be ready and expecting it. So this is what your interviewer will do:

1 They'll start by welcoming you, and will probably chat for a couple of minutes to put you at your ease. They may well offer you a coffee or tea.

2 They will start the interview proper by asking you the list of general questions which they are asking every candidate. These will be questions like, 'Tell me about yourself' or, 'What is your experience of working to deadlines?'

3 Next, they'll ask you specific questions arising from your own application form or CV. These will be questions such as, 'I see you've only been with your current employer six months. Why are you looking for another job so soon?' or, 'I see you list Antarctic exploration among your hobbies. How do you find this fits in with a nine-to-five job?'

4 After this, they may come back to earlier points and probe further if they're still concerned (we'll look at this in a moment).

5 Finally, when they've worked through all their questions, they will fill you in on a few more details about the job, and then ask you for your questions.

---

**Did you know?**

Interviewers are trained to make sure that they do only about 20 to 30 per cent of the talking during the interview – until the final stage. This means they'll be expecting you to do 70 to 80 per cent of the talking.

---

# Reassuring the interviewer

If your interviewer has a niggling worry about something in your application that makes them think you may not be able to do the job, what are they going to do? If they know their job, they'll probe until they get a satisfactory answer from you. And thet's the way you want it.

If they don't ask you questions, the likely result is that they won't offer you the job because they are concerned, for example, about the 18-month gap in your CV. They are worried that you were unable to get work because of poor references, or lack of ability. But in fact, you might have taken 18 months off to look after a sick relative, or to have a baby. If the interviewer doesn't ask, you can't reassure them that the employment gap is no reflection on your ability to do this job.

Now, some interviewers find it easy to probe these areas of concern. But others are less assertive and worry that they may offend or upset you. They shouldn't do, because you should be grateful for the chance to reassure them. But in case your interviewer is reticent, be ready to pick up their hints and fill them in on the facts. Otherwise neither of you may address the issue full on, and you could end up missing out on the job because of some unfounded worry on the interviewer's part.

## So what sets off alarm bells for interviewers?

We asked several professional interviewers to tell us what gets them most worried on an application form. If any of these appear on your application form you need to be ready to counter them. The interviewers told us they worry if they see evidence of:

- lack of relevant experience (so you need to make sure that every relevant piece of experience is clearly highlighted)

- lack of relevant personal attributes such as the ability to work under pressure, for example, or to motivate others (so look at what is needed in this job and show that you've got it)

- slower progress up the career ladder than they would expect (so have an explanation for it. such as you slowed down your career when your family was young, or you turned down promotion for a good reason)

- employment gaps (so make it clear what you were doing during these gaps and why that experience has helped to fit you for this job).

You may be wondering what you're supposed to do if the concern is well founded. Suppose you really do lack the experience they need, or you did spend a year out of work because you couldn't get a job. In this case, the most important thing you can do is be ready for the question. Look through your application and CV and work out where the interviewer's concerns will lie. Then you can prepare answers to the questions.

In general, the way to answer these questions – when they are genuine – is to be honest but give plenty of compensating factors. If you genuinely lack experience admit to it, but demonstrate that you are a fast learner and can learn on the job. And that you believe your strengths outweigh this weakness in any case.

# Internal applicants

If you're applying for a job within your own organization, can you expect the interview to follow the same format? Yes, you can. The interviewer can only assess all the candidates equally if they have interviewed them all on an equal basis. That means everyone should be allocated the same amount of time, given the same level of respect and privacy, and asked the same questions – whether they are internal or external applicants.

What's more, just because your interviewer may know the answer to some of the questions already, for example 'How well do you work under pressure?', they still want to hear your answer to the question. So don't say 'That's a stupid question, you know that already', just give them the answer you would if this were an external interview.

### Did you know?

There is a growing trend for employers to advertise internal vacancies, rather than simply offer the job to whoever they decide they want to appoint. So you are increasingly likely to find that for internal promotion, you have to go through an internal application and interview process.

So you can expect the interviewer to follow exactly the same format, if you are an internal applicant whom they already know, as they would if you were applying from outside the organization. However, you don't have to pretend you've never met before. They will lead the opening minute or two of chat, and they're likely to behave as they normally do rather than pretend you're a stranger; this will help to set the tone.

Don't make a big thing of your internal status, cracking in-jokes or being personal – even in a positive way – about colleagues. But there's no need to pretend the interviewer doesn't know what you're talking about when they do. You may find it helps to answer questions as you would at an outside interview, but add phrases such as 'You'll remember …', or 'As you know …'.

## Prepare for the expected

You can get ready for this interview by knowing what the interviewer is looking for, and making sure that you are ready to prove that you've got it:

■ Assess yourself for the job in the key areas of skills, experience and so on.

■ Consider the key areas on your application form and CV that they are likely to want to ask you about.

■ Think about whether your CV or application shows up anything which might – rightly or wrongly – give your interviewer cause to worry about your ability to do the job.

# 2 How to prepare

It would be deeply unwise, as I'm sure you don't need telling, to walk straight into an important interview without doing any preparation in advance. The better prepared you are, the better your chances of winning the job. Of course, you've already worked on your application form and your CV in order to get this far. But having made it through to Round Two, it's time for some more homework.

**Just imagine...**

... you've done little or no preparation and you're sitting in the interview. The interviewer asks you, 'What can you tell me about this company?' And you realize that apart from what industry it's in, and the address (because you're there right now), you can't answer the question. How would you feel?

**Whoops...**

Essentially, you have to see yourself as a salesperson, and do the preparation a salesperson would do before winning a big contract. Yes, even if the job you're applying for has nothing to do with selling. The point is that you are selling yourself, and your interviewer is taking the role of buyer. The buyer will look at what you – and the competition – have to offer, and will then make their buying decision. Your job is to persuade them that you are a better buy than your competitors.

A salesperson would never visit a buyer without thorough preparation for the meeting, and nor should you. So you will need to:

- Set your objective.
- Research the organization you're applying to.
- Prepare your own case.
- Be prepared for the interview.

# Set your objective

An objective is a destination. If you don't know exactly where you're headed, it's unlikely that you'll get there with any efficiency. And you may not get there at all. You might think your objective is obvious: to get the job. Well, you'd be right. And wrong. That tells you where you're going, but it doesn't tell you how you're going to get there. And just as a well-planned journey needs a route as well as a destination, so a well-planned objective needs to tell you not only where you're going, but also how you're going to get there.

## Selection savvy

Once you've set your objective it won't vary much from one job to the next. But look at it afresh for each job you apply for, to make sure you keep your preparation focused right where it needs to be.

So how are you going to get the job? Here's a more specific objective for you: *to get the job by demonstrating to the interviewer that I am the best person for it.* Well, yes, that's better. But it still doesn't tell you everything. That's like saying you're going to go to Manchester via Birmingham, but not giving any clues as to which roads will take you there.

OK, let's try again: *to get the job by demonstrating to the interviewer that I am the best person for it in terms of ability, experience and personality.* Now we're getting somewhere. And if you have any more information you can add, in terms of the interviewer's specific priorities, you can add this to your objective. Perhaps you know that what the interviewer really wants is someone with experience of negotiating with suppliers.

In that case, your objective should reflect this: *to get the job by demonstrating to the interviewer that I am the best person for it in terms of ability, experience and personality, and in particular at negotiating with suppliers.* That's great. A clear, specific objective. That will be really useful.

Umm … useful? An objective? It all looks very professional, but quite how is it going to help? Well, it's easy to fall into the trap of thinking that objectives are a waste of time. So many people formulate them and then ignore them that one's perception is, quite rightly, that they might as well not bother. But if you're smart, you'll use your objective, and then you'll find out how valuable it can be.

You see, a clear, well-conceived objective is a touchstone against which you can measure everything you do. It helps to keep you focused. If any activity doesn't help you meet your objective, don't do it. Use the time for something that *will* further it. For example, we're about to look at researching the organization to which you're applying. You need to do enough research to demonstrate that you've done your homework, but beyond that, what do you need to find out?

The answer is, you need to find out anything that helps meet your objective, and nothing else. So to take our earlier example: *to get the job by demonstrating to the interviewer that I am the best person for it in terms of ability, experience and personality, and in particular at negotiating with suppliers*, you need to focus your efforts in finding out about their suppliers: how many are there, who are they, and so on.

---

**On course: yes or no?**

Taking the objective: *to get the job by demonstrating to the interviewer that I am the best person for it in terms of ability, experience and personality, and in particular at handling difficult customers*, which of the following preparation activities do you think meet the objective?

| Activity | Yes | No |
|---|---|---|
| 1 Obtain reference for voluntary work as a Samaritan. | | |
| 2 Memorize company's annual report and financial documents. | | |
| 3 Dig out school GCSE certificates from 1994. | | |
| 4 Dig out copies of letters of appreciation from customers. | | |
| 5 List experience of dealing with difficult people in general. | | |

*Answers:* Yes: 1,4,5  No: 2,3

---

It's not that it's impossible to arrive at this conclusion – about, for example, where to focus your research – without an objective. But having an objective, and just going through the process of generating it, will help to concentrate your mind on the essential areas and help it to keep coming back to them. It will prevent you becoming distracted from your core aim.

# Research the organization

The interviewer will expect you to have done some research into the organization. It's not that they want to catch you out with difficult questions – if that's their aim they can come up with plenty of other ways of achieving it. It's just that they want to see that you are:

- putting some effort into winning this job
- interested in the organization
- showing enthusiasm.

If these are all genuinely the case, you'll want to research the organization. How can you be sure you want to work there, if you're offered the job, unless you know something about the place? The interviewer is likely to ask you a few questions about what you know of their company, just to make sure you've shown enthusiasm, interest and effort.

## Selection savvy

Don't simply research the organization in isolation – look at the whole industry. See where it fits in, who its main competitors are, and look at industry trends and so on as well. That way you can show the interviewer that you understand the big picture too.

So what material can you get hold of to help you find out about the organization? Here are a few ideas:

- annual report
- sales brochures
- customer newsletter
- in-house magazine
- newspaper and trade magazine articles.

You might be able to find this information in all sorts of ways. Maybe you know someone who works at the organization, or perhaps there are retail outlets where you can pick up material. But by far the simplest approach is to phone and ask for it.

The interviewer isn't trying to trick you. They don't want to make it hard for you. So just call them (or a secretary or assistant) and say 'I'd like to find out a bit more about the organization before I come for my interview. Please could you send me some information?' They'll be happy to do so, and impressed at your initiative.

## Did you know?

Over 96 per cent of organisations now have a website. Even among small businesses with a turnover of less than £1 million, well over half have websites. So go online – use an internet café if you have no other web access – and check out your prospective employer's website for all sorts of information about them.

Source: Summer 2000 Marketing Trends Survey
Chartered Institute of Marketing,
*www.marketingportal.cim.co.uk*

Now, once you've got your hands on this information, what are you going to do with it? The answer is that you're going to sift through it looking for clues to showing that you are the best person for the job – bearing in mind your objective, of course. For example:

- Suppose you notice that the company does a lot of business with Latin America. And you speak excellent Spanish. That will give you an advantage over most, if not all, the other applicants.

- Or perhaps you can see that the company is growing fast. The same goes for the company you're with now, and you know it can cause all sorts of problems for the IT department (where you're applying to work). You've been through it all already and you know how to overcome the difficulties.

- Maybe the latest issue of the in-house newsletter is putting out a call for editorial help, and you've edited a company magazine in the past.

You should be able to find a good few opportunities to display how well suited you are to the job as you look through the material you've acquired.

**Selection savvy**

Don't wait to be asked what you know about the company. If you find opportunities throughout the interview to say, for example, 'I speak fluent Spanish. And I notice you do a lot of business with South American countries, so I imagine that will be very useful', you'll impress the interviewer with your research – as well as your relevant skills – as you go along. The more relevant facts about their company you can include during the interview, the better. They won't need to ask if you've done your research. It will be obvious.

# Prepare your own case

If you simply walk into the interview and answer each question as it's asked, without having done any preparation, you'll probably put on a fairly decent show. But if you really want this job, that's not enough. You have no idea how tough the competition is. If it's fairly weak, an unprepared interview might still get you the job. But what if it's strong? A missed opportunity – something you might have said but forgot to mention – might tip the balance against you.

So we've got to make sure it doesn't happen. Before you get to the interview, you should already have a mental list of all the most important points you want to make – all the things that will impress on your interviewer that you are the best person for the job.

You've already assessed yourself to establish what your key strengths are. You're going to want to drive these home. If your strengths can be objectively measured – qualifications, skill at using particular equipment, that sort of thing – simply telling the interviewer that you possess them will be sufficient. But some strengths – such as experience or diplomacy skills, for example – will need to be illustrated with examples.

So think of examples in advance of the interview. Suppose you consider diplomacy to be one of your key skills. And your objective tells you that it is one of the things you have to persuade your interviewer that you are good at. When they ask you about it (and they will if it's one of their key requirements for the job), it's not enough simply to assure them that it's something you're good at. Even if it was important in your last job, that doesn't prove you were good at that part of the job.

No, you need to give them strong examples. Tell them about the time an angry customer stormed into the store throwing tomatoes at all the staff, and you calmed them down. Or about the time the entire team of delivery drivers was about to stage a walkout, until you talked to them. Tell them about both if you get the chance.

## Just imagine...

... one of the key requirements of the job is the ability to lead a team of people. You've had very little managerial experience, but you tell the interviewer that you've had one full timer and one part timer working under you for the last year. After you've left the interview, you realize you completely forgot to mention that when you were in your last job, you also organized trade show appearances, which involved running a team for a week or two several times a year.

Meanwhile ... one of the other candidates has as little professional experience as you of managing a permanent team, but has told the interviewer all about how their present job entails leading a team of outside caterers, cleaners and other helpers whenever they hold events such as product launches.

### Whoops...

You may be able to think of an example to illustrate your strengths on the spot when you're asked. But if you prepare in advance you won't just come up with any example, you'll come up with the best, and the most relevant to the job you're applying for.

So that's your basic list of strengths. And you also need to go through the job description in much the same way, finding examples to demonstrate that you have experience in all the key areas of responsibility. If you don't have a copy of the job description (which would normally be sent out with the application form) phone the interviewer's office and ask them to send you one. It's standard practice, so they won't mind being asked.

## Selection savvy

When you're looking for examples of past experience to show that you can handle all the key responsibilities, don't restrict yourself to work experience – you may be able to demonstrate your motivational skills by explaining how you organize volunteers at a local charity you work for. Perhaps you can demonstrate your ability to work to deadlines by telling the interviewer about the school magazine you edited. Or you might indicate self-motivation and commitment by talking about your Open University degree.

Your interviewer might be interested to see some evidence to back up any strengths and experience that you tell them about. While they are unlikely to expect to see anything other than perhaps proof of qualifications, they may well be impressed by anything else you can offer them such as:

- testimonials from satisfied customers or suppliers
- copies of key reports you've written
- examples of past work
- press cuttings you've generated
- press articles about events you've organised

… and the like. So find anything you can which will help to persuade them that you really are as good as you look, and take it along. Clearly it's not a good idea to turn up at the interview pushing a wheelbarrow of stuff in front of you. Take what's portable, and will fit into a neat folder – or a portfolio if it involves a lot of design or artwork. Then let the interviewer know what else you could send them – or bring to a second interview – if they want to see it.

# Be prepared for the interview

You know what you want to say at the interview now. Whatever questions the interviewer puts to you, there are certain key points which you want to get across and which you have prepared. But how long have you got to say them? Have you got to cram your key selling points into 15 minutes, or have you got an hour to bring them out slowly, one by one?

The only way you can find out the answer to this is by asking. So you need to contact your interviewer's office (preferably at the same time as any other requests you have to make) and simply ask, 'Please could you tell me how much time has been allocated to my interview?' Again, it's a totally reasonable question, and one they should be happy to answer.

You now have all the advance information you need, and all your preparation is in place. The final step is to be ready for the interview on the day itself. And you can start by being on time. It doesn't matter how early you arrive – you can always find the building and then go for a walk, for lunch or for a browse in the local shops so you don't arrive at reception too soon. But being as little as two or three minutes late may matter a lot – especially if your interviewer turns out to be a stickler for good time-keeping.

**Just imagine...**

... the stuff of nightmares. You leave on time but the train is cancelled or your car breaks down. Or maybe the travelling is OK but you can't find the building. Having arrived in the vicinity half an hour early, the minutes are ticking away and you can't find the building. Or perhaps you turn up 20 minutes early for your 2 o'clock interview, only to discover that the letter you hadn't looked at recently says 12 o'clock, not 2.

**Whoops...**

Of course you can imagine scenarios where no amount of forward planning could have got you to the interview on time. But unless the reason is highly dramatic, you interviewer doesn't want to hear excuses. They just want you to be there on time. So do yourself a few favours:

- Leave plenty of time to get there.
- Take with you the letter inviting you to the interview, with the time on it, and any directions you've been sent.
- Enquire about parking if you're travelling by car and think it could be a problem.
- Take a mobile phone, or money for phone calls, in case you need to ring for directions. Then if you do still run late, despite all your precautions, at least you can phone ahead and let them know what's happening.

As well as making sure you arrive on time, you will also need to take with you:

- your portfolio material as well as directions, mobile phone and anything else – all neatly in one briefcase.
- a notepad and pen (also in the briefcase) for jotting down notes during the interview.

## Do your homework

A couple of weeks before the interview, phone the interviewer's office if necessary to ask for:

- any information they can give you about the organization
- the job description
- an idea of how much time has been allocated for the interview.

Use other sources as well, including their website, to find out what you can about the company. Look through this information and find anything you can which will both show you've done your research, and demonstrate that you're the best person for the job.

Go through your list of strengths, and the key responsibilities listed on the job description, and think of concrete examples to demonstrate your strengths and abilities as well as you can. Put together a portfolio of relevant and useful material to take to the interview.

Leave plenty of time to get to the interview, and make sure you remember to take with you everything you might need.

# 3 First impressions

Your interviewer will form a frighteningly large part of their opinion of you on the basis of a very small proportion of the time they spend with you. In fact, the first few moments will tell them a great deal about you, whether you like it or not. Your best defence against this, of course, is to make sure you send out the messages you want.

From the way you dress to the way you say hello, you can prepare yourself to give the best possible first impression. In fact, why not start before you even get to the day of the interview? You can influence your interviewer's opinion:

- before the interview
- in the way you dress
- by the way you greet them.

When surveyed, interviewers cited the following among the key factors that impress them about a candidate:

- strong handshake

- being smartly and appropriately dressed.

Factors that impress them least included:

- lateness

- sloppy appearance

- poor grooming

- too much perfume or aftershave.

# Before the interview

Yes, even before you get to the interview, you can already be generating a strong first impression. Your original application was clearly good enough to win you an interview. If it included a really well-presented and professional looking CV and application form, your interviewer will already be expecting a strong candidate to walk through the door. You can enhance this impression even further with:

- a well-written covering letter when you sent in your application, briefly outlining your strengths (in relation to the job in question)

- a further letter, again well written and professionally laid out, confirming the arrangements for this interview and saying how much you are looking forward to it.

If it's too late for these now, you can still give a great first impression. But next time you apply for a job, bear these points in mind so you can make a strong, positive impression even before the interview.

# What are you going to wear?

Knowing how to dress for an interview ain't what it used to be. Time was, you put on your best suit and tie, or your smartest tailored dress or skirt suit, and you knew you looked the part. Unfortunately, things aren't so simple any more. A smart, formal outfit just won't look right in an organization where the workforce all wear jeans and T-shirts. The interviewer will think, 'Very smart. They'll never fit in here.'

### Did you know?

According to research, as much as 70 per cent of employee turnover is due to staff not fitting in with the corporate culture, rather than an inability to do the job in terms of skills or experience. So your interviewer wants to see that you will fit in if they offer you the job. The way you dress is only a part of this, of course, but it is a large part of the interviewer's first impression of whether or not you are 'one of us'.

So you need to know what the dress code is at the organization you're applying to. That way you can pick an appropriate outfit (as we'll see in a minute). You may well have a pretty clear idea of what the dress code is likely to be; it is often fairly consistent across whole industries. Design and media companies tend to dress casually, accountancy firms are likely to dress smarter. If you're changing jobs within your own industry, the odds are you'll be pretty clear about the usual style.

But what if this is an industry you're not so sure about? There are several options:

- If you're lucky enough to know someone who works for the organization – or simply knows them as a supplier or a customer perhaps – you can ask their advice.

- If the organization is based nearby, turn up at lunchtime or going home time and watch people leaving the building to see what they are all wearing.

- Look through sales brochures and annual reports for photos of management and staff.

But failing all that, the answer is the same as usual: ask. When you're phoning your contact – the interviewer, their assistant or their secretary – ask them what the company dress code is. As always, they won't mind being asked, they'll be impressed at your initiative.

So what to wear, then? Just because you've found out what the regular employees wear, doesn't mean you're going to wear the same thing yourself. Sorry – it's not quite that simple. After all, you're not a regular employee (yet); you're an interviewee who needs to look as if they're making an extra effort. So dress a notch or two above the employees – look like they would if they were making an effort. So for men:

| If they wear ... | You wear ... |
|---|---|
| Casual | Smart casual |
| Smart casual | Casual suit |
| Casual suit (e.g. shirtsleeves, or no tie) | Casual suit with a jacket and tie |
| Smart suit | Smart suit |

And for women:

| If they wear ... | You wear... |
|---|---|
| Casual | Smart casual (e.g. trousers, but not jeans) |
| Smart casual | Smart |
| Smart | Smart |

That makes it look a little simpler for women. In a sense it is, because there's more of a sliding scale. For men, either it's OK to remove your jacket, for example, or it isn't. But the point is the same: dress a notch or two above the people you'll be passing in the corridor when you go to the interview, unless they're already formally dressed, in which case you need only match them (rather than turning up in full evening dress).

## Selection savvy

Whatever you do, don't go out and buy a new outfit for your interview, unless you have plenty of time to break it in first. You need to be comfortable and relaxed, concentrating on the conversation, not on the zip that you've just discovered sticks into you painfully, or the waistband which felt fine when you tried the thing on in the shop, but turns out to be much too tight when you sit down. Pick clothes which are clean and smart, and relatively new, but ones which you know are comfortable and problem-free.

When it comes to the specifics of the outfit you choose to wear, here are a few more pointers you may find useful:

- Don't let your appearance overpower your personality. You can wear bright colours, but don't wear something so unusual it steals all the attention. It's you applying for this job, not your clothes.
- Avoid any extremes of fashion.
- Avoid strong perfume or aftershave.
- Don't wear too much jewellery, or jewellery that is too large.
- Avoid large patterns in bright colours, unless restricted to a small area such as a tie or scarf.
- Dark colours will lend you more authority than pale ones.

When you arrive for the interview – a few minutes early – ask the receptionist to direct you to somewhere where you can freshen up. Tidy your hair and check your clothes, and double check your:

- teeth (especially if you've been eating)
- nose
- jewellery (especially earrings for women)
- zips and buttons (especially flies for men)
- shirt or blouse (make sure they are tucked in)
- make-up.

It is worthwhile, if you're a woman, taking a spare pair of tights (if you're wearing tights). Likewise, if you're a man, it's worth bringing along a spare tie in case you spill food or drink down the first one. Or just don't put your tie on until you reach the building.

## Your opening greeting

As well as the way you look, the way you greet the interviewer will also be an important part of the first impression you create. So be ready to exude warmth and confidence as soon as you see them. The key points to remember are:

- Smile.
- Make eye contact with the interviewer.
- Offer a hand to shake as soon as they introduce themselves.
- Say 'Hello', 'Pleased to meet you', or whatever phrase you feel easy with.
- Shake hands firmly (you can practise your handshake with a friend) – with all the interviewers if there is more than one.
- Wait to be invited before sitting down.

### Selection savvy

Many interviewers want an informal second opinion on candidates from one or more members of their team (after all, they'll have to work with whoever gets the job). So they may ask a team member to greet you at reception, give you a cup of coffee, or conduct you from reception to the interview room – and back again afterwards. In other words, you need to make as good a first impression as you can on *everyone* you meet – including the receptionist – because you don't know which of them may have an input into the final selection.

### 4 things to say on the way to the interview room

Sometimes you're met by the interviewer or an assistant at reception. Then you have to make polite conversation along what might be miles of corridor to the interview room. What do you say? Here are some ideas:

■ If they ask you a question such as 'How was your journey?' give a positive answer (even if the journey was awful). And don't be mono-syllabic. You could say something like, 'Oh, it was fine, thanks. Much quicker than I thought and the parking was very straightfor-ward.'

■ If they don't ask, volunteer how your journey was: 'It was easy to get here. That map in the brochure you sent me is very clear.' Or, 'What are they doing at the end of the street? There's quite a traffic jam there and I noticed some huge building project as I passed.'

■ Ask them, 'How long have you worked for this organization?' People always like you to show an interest in them personally.

■ Make a favourable comment about something you're passing: 'What a great view from these windows!' or 'This is a really bright, modern building. How long has it been here?'

The interviewer will generally chat for a minute or two at the start to put you at your ease. Be responsive, but remember that neither of you is here to chat. So when they ask, for example, how your journey was, they don't want a blow-by-blow account of it. A friendly but brief response will do fine. And if by any chance it was horrendous, express the fact (if you mention it at all) with humour rather than sounding like a whinger.

## Make your mark

Before the interview, give a strong first impression with a well-written and presented application, and a letter confirming the interview and saying that you are looking forward to it.

Choose an outfit which will suit the company culture, and is a notch or two smarter than the regular employees wear. Give a warm, friendly and confident greeting to your interviewer, and anyone else you meet from the organization.

# part two

# during
## the
## interview

# 4 Coping with nerves

Almost all of us feel nervous before an important interview. After all, it's something that matters to us that we need to get right. So nerves are only natural. But of course there's a world of difference between a little shot of adrenalin that keeps you on your toes, and a paralyzing numbness that dries your mouth out, makes you sweat copiously, and renders you incapable of answering any questions.

In fact, most of us fall between these two extremes. But if you're one of the people who find that nerves get in the way of a good interview, what can you do about it? Well, you'll be pleased to know that almost all cases of severe nerves can be reduced to a manageable level, and the less severe cases can all but disappear. It just takes preparation.

## what the experts say

Interviewers don't consider nerves a problem at all, so long as they don't get significantly worse during the interview. Comments on the subject from professional intervewers include:

- 'If a candidate is nervous it is up to the interviewer to relax them.'

- 'They are obviously interested in the position or they would not be nervous.'

# Root of the problem

The key lies in understanding what causes an attack of nerves. And the root cause is fear. Fear of what could go wrong, from drying up completely to soaking the interviewer by spilling your coffee. The more remote these failures and catastrophes seem, the more remote will be your fears. This is why you often notice a couple of minutes into an interview that you're not nearly as nervous as you were just before you began: things are going fine, you realize you're not making a prat of yourself and you seem to be able to hold a normal conversation after all.

## Selection savvy

What do you do if something really goes catastrophically wrong? You spill water all down yourself, or knock a huge pile of papers across the floor. Or maybe you're so nervous you can't remember the name of your current employer. It's not likely to happen after you've read this chapter, but just supposing …

The answer is to laugh at yourself, and admit to being nervous. Say something like, 'That's what nerves can do to you! It shows how important this job is to me.' Unless you're being interviewed for a post where you're going to have to give huge presentations or entertain famous celebrities, there's no reason why your interviewer should count it against you, so long as you show you can respond well and with humour.

If you can minimize the likelihood of things going wrong, you will minimize your fears. Of course there will still be a small irrational panic at the very back of your mind, at least until the interview is under way, but it need cause no more than a touch of adrenalin which simply keeps you thinking fast.

Your best bet is to rehearse as thoroughly as you can. Think through your replies to likely questions and tough ones (you'll find them later in the book), and practise your answers in front of a mirror. Rehearse your opening greeting. Try your outfit on in advance if you haven't worn it recently.

But you will still want to take other precautions. Your motto should be: be prepared. Anticipate disaster, consider every possible emergency or embarrassment you can, and plan for it. That way, it won't happen or – even if it does – you'll be ready to cope. Here are some antidotes to one or two classic adrenalin-starters:

| | |
|---|---|
| **Coffee and tea** | If you're worried you'll spill them, simply decline them when offered. In fact, caffeine's not a great idea anyway if you're nervous – avoid it for the previous couple of hours too (along with any form of alcohol). If you're prone to shake when you're nervous, best decline a drink as the shakiness will really show when you pick it up. |
| **Looking nervous** | Actually, no one cares if you look nervous so long as you still do the job well. But we often fear appearing to be nervous. If you are inclined to shake at the start of the interview, fold your hands together in your lap where they can keep each other under control. |
| **Mouth turning dry** | When you turn down the coffee, ask for a glass of water instead. If you don't need it, it's OK to leave it (you don't have to drink it and have the worry of spilling it). |
| **Unable to think of anything to say** | Here's another time the glass of water comes in handy. Taking a sip or two before you answer a question buys you a few moments to get your head straight. |
| **Fumbling with briefcase/spilling papers** | Take into the interview just a single envelope file. Leave the rest of your stuff at reception. |

**Difficult questions**    Get someone to role play a question and answer session with you and brief them to be as difficult as possible. That way, the real thing will be a breeze by comparison.

# Easing the symptoms

As far as coping with the physical symptoms of nerves is concerned, try to eat before the interview. Don't binge, but a light breakfast or lunch will help (unless you honestly think you'll bring it straight back up). Nerves are always worse on an empty stomach.

You may also find relaxation exercises helpful. The way to reduce stress is to relax, and slow breathing is a quick fix for this. Here's an exercise which you can do moments before your interview, for example while you're waiting at reception:

---

**Relaxation exercise**

1 Sit down if possible, but you can do this standing up if necessary.

2 Relax your arms and hands. If you're sitting down, put your hands in your lap.

3 Close your eyes if you can, but again this isn't essential.

4 Breathe in through your nose, slowly, to a count of five. Breathe in as low down as you can, pushing out your diaphragm and stomach.

5 Breathe out through your mouth to a count of seven. If you are sitting down, don't slump as you breathe out.

6 Allow your breathing to return to normal and open your eyes.

You can repeat this at intervals as often as you need to, but always let your breathing return to normal in between. If you don't, you may hyperventilate. This won't do you any harm, but it can make you feel a little light headed which may make you more nervous rather than more relaxed.

Even once the interview is under way, there are still techniques you can use on the spot to help you relax:

- Take a deep breath while the interviewer is asking you a question. The more tense we get, the more our ribs and chest lock up. By releasing them with a deep, chest-expanding breath, you ease the tension so it can't build up. This requires no concentration, so you can still focus on what the interviewer is asking you.

- Smiling helps to relax your muscles. You may feel like an idiot if you grin inanely throughout the interview, but if you can find opportunities to smile as you begin to respond to a question it will relax you. And it will help you come across as a warm and friendly person, too.

- If you notice yourself sitting hunched up, legs and arms crossed (not to mention fingers), shift to a more open and relaxed position. We'll be looking at body language in the next chapter, but the important thing for relaxation is just to open up and allow your muscles to relax.

Your muscles may tense up as a result of psychological nervousness, but you can reverse the cause and effect: relaxing your muscles can make you feel less nervous.

### Relax!

Prepare yourself as much as you can for the interview. The more you have rehearsed and prepared, the less you have to fear. And the less you have to fear, the less nervous you will feel. So:

- Practise your responses.
- Plan to avoid or cope with the biggest adrenalin-starters.
- Use simple relaxation techniques to ease nerves on the day.

# 5 Projecting the right image

We've already established the importance of first impressions. But it doesn't stop there, of course. You have to continue to give the best possible impression throughout the interview. Quite apart from what you say, the way you say it will have a big impact on your interviewer's opinion of you – and of whether you're the best person for the job.

This doesn't mean you have to do a crash course in acting at your local drama school, and transform yourself into someone completely different. There's no need to put on an act – just be yourself. But your natural personality will have many different qualities, and you need to make sure it is the positive and relevant ones which stand out at interview. So projecting the right image is about being you, but using the behaviours which will most impress your interviewer.

---

### Spot check

Here's a quick test. See if you can tell which qualities most influence interviewers, according to a survey by Career World. Put them in order of importance:

- your personality, how you present yourself in the interview
- your experience
- the qualifications you have for the position
- your background and references
- the enthusiasm you have towards the organization and position.

---

It's worth reinforcing that all five of these qualities are important, and you need to demonstrate your suitability in each area. But what's the right priority? In fact, the order they are listed in above is the order of importance in which interviewers placed them. Yep, how you come across in the interview is the single most important factor in whether you get the job. So what do you need to do?

# Essential qualities

There are a few essential qualities you need to project.

## Be responsive

Make an effort to give full (but not rambling) answers to your interviewer's questions, and to volunteer relevant information. Don't give one-word answers – they sound sullen and unhelpful, even if that's not your intention. So if they say, 'I see you trained originally in marketing?' don't just say, 'Yes'. Answer, for example, 'Yes, I did. But in my first marketing job I did a lot of PR work, and particularly enjoyed the press side of it, so I decided to specialize in press relations.'

## Be confident

You may be feeling anything but confident, but confidence is an attractive quality in an employee so you need to show you have it. Research shows that interviewers just don't like giving jobs to people who put themselves down. Of course, this doesn't mean you should be pushy and arrogant, but don't apologize for yourself. If your interviewer says, 'So it's two years since you did any actual face-to-face selling', don't say, 'I'm afraid so'. Say something like, 'It is, but I always feel it's one of those skills that you never lose once you've learnt it.'

**Just imagine...**

... you've got all the right experience, and your qualifications are better than any of the other applicants. You have brilliant references and you've done your research – and it shows. There's just one problem. You give the impression that you don't believe in yourself. You keep saying things like, 'I'm sorry, I haven't got much experience of that software. I've only been using it for a few months' (when you could have said, 'Sure, I know it well. I've been using it for the last few months'). In the end, the interviewer comes to share your low opinion of yourself, and the job goes to someone else.

**Whoops...**

## Be energetic

People who project life and energy come across as so much more positive, capable and even inspiring than those who seem flat and sluggish. So stay upbeat, sit up straight, speak clearly and make eye contact (with all your interviewers if there's more than one).

## Be enthusiastic

This is closely related to being energetic, and goes alongside it. We've seen that enthusiasm towards the job and the position is important to interviewers (yes, I know it was number five on the list, but they were *all* important). The best way to transmit this enthusiasm is by seeming interested in what both you and the interviewer are saying. If you genuinely are interested, you shouldn't find this too difficult – just make sure you let it show.

It never helps your image to smoke in an interview, and it often harms it. Even if your interviewer is a smoker and offers you a cigarette, decline it. Smoking can give you an air of being too informal, laid back and relaxed – good qualities in general, but you should appear more keen to make a good impression at an interview that is important to you. Alternatively, a cigarette may make you appear nervous and neurotic; again, not the way you want to come across.

# Body language

The way you come across visually can be as important as the way you come across verbally. And in fact, your body language can affect your verbal communication too. Here's an interesting exercise for you.

### Cause and effect

- Sit on a chair and fold your arms.
- Cross your legs.
- Slump in the chair.
- Now imagine you're at an interview and the interviewer is sitting in front of you. Don't look at them – stare at the floor instead.
- Don't allow yourself to use any facial expressions.
- Now answer – out loud – the question: 'What do you enjoy most about your present job?'

That was Part 1 of the exercise. Now for Part 2:

- Relax your hands in your lap.
- Put both feet on the floor.
- Don't slump, but lean slightly forwards.
- Look straight at your imaginary interviewer.
- Smile.
- Now answer – out loud – the question: 'What do you enjoy most about your present job?'

You should find that there is a marked difference in your tone as you answer the question using these two, very different physical approaches. When you adopt positive, upbeat body language (Part 2, as I'm sure you realize) your whole tone lifts, and sounds more confident, energetic and enthusiastic – all qualities that we've just established you need to project.

You'll find, just as we saw earlier with relaxing your body to ease nerves, that the cause and effect can work both ways. If you are positive and upbeat, your body language will largely follow. Or start with the body language – get that right and you will become more positive and upbeat.

So it's worth knowing what the optimum body language signals are, but don't get hung up on them. If you're projecting the right qualities, and feeling the appropriate emotions, the body language will follow naturally. But if you sense that you are flagging, that you sound less positive than you would like to, you can monitor your body language and adapt it in order to lift your mood and your verbal tone.

Professional interviewers say that good eye contact from the candidate is essential to giving them a good impression.

So what are the essential points of body language to project during an interview? Here are the most important things to bear in mind:

- Don't perch on the edge of your chair. Sit well back in it – unless it's a very deep, upholstered chair in which case there's a danger of looking too relaxed if you get lost right in the back of it.

- Sit with both feet on the floor, leaning slightly towards the interviewer.

- Make frequent eye contact with the interviewer. If there is more than one of them, make eye contact with them all but look chiefly at whichever one asked the question you are answering.

- Smile readily.

- Don't hide your face with your hands.

- Don't give off defensive signals by crossing your arms and your legs.

- Try to keep your hands still except when you're gesturing. Don't play with your hair or put your hands in your pockets.

**Candidate with attitude**

Once you've successfully made a good first impression, I'm afraid you can't let up. You need to consolidate your good work by continuing to project a strong positive image. So be:

- responsive
- confident
- energetic
- enthusiastic.

And remember to monitor your body language (without getting distracted from answering the interviewer's questions). In particular, change your body language if you feel you are sounding lethargic, unenthusiastic or downbeat.

# 6 The interview

We've already established the format that the interview is likely to take. Just to recap:

1 After an initial brief chat, the interviewer will ask you questions from a general list that all candidates are being asked.

2 Then they will ask you questions arising from your own particular application. The questions, obviously, are the bulk of the interview, and we'll be looking at them in more detail in the next couple of chapters.

3 After this, the interviewer will probably tell you a bit more about the organization and the job.

4 Finally, they will ask for your questions.

Knowing the format to expect is a big help. But you still need to know how to handle the interview professionally in general terms. So we'll take a look at the broad points of your interview style, the sort of questions to be ready for, and how to deal with different types of interview such as panel or telephone interviews. Finally, making a good exit is almost as important as making a good entrance, so we'll see how to wind up an interview cleanly and smartly.

## Interview style

Apart from answering the questions as positively as you can, there are a few other skills that will help you impress your interviewer (or avoid putting them off you). The manner in which you answer questions can be as important as the answers you give, so you need to deliver the whole package.

■ Make sure you speak clearly, and answer questions without mumbling. Good body language and eye contact will help you to do this naturally.

■ Don't interrupt the interviewer – even if they interrupt you.

■ Apart from asking for clarification of a question if you need to, avoid asking more than a few brief questions at most during the interview. This is the interviewer's time to question you – you'll get a chance to ask them questions later on.

■ Adopt a similar tone to the interviewer. If they are very formal, you need to follow suit. Be very wary of anything more than gentle humour unless your interviewer is injecting a lot of humour into the conversation (in which case laugh politely at their jokes).

■ Don't ask your interviewer questions about salary. It looks as though you're only interested in the money. If they offer you the job, there'll be plenty of time to discuss the salary later (negotiating your starting package is covered in Part 3 of this book).

## Selection savvy

Many people feel uncomfortable about blowing their own trumpet. It seems arrogant to say 'I'm brilliant at this' or 'The project would have fallen apart without my foresight in spotting pitfalls'. You don't have to say any of these things. Just state the facts, and the interviewer will draw the right conclusions for themselves. Give strong examples of your work, which demonstrate your strengths without having to spell them out in such strong language.

# Responding positively

The next couple of chapters deal with specific questions, but there are certain general guidelines for answering any question which you'll need to follow. All of these are aimed at giving the interviewer a positive view of you as someone who is confident, capable and honest.

■ *Don't ramble.* Aim for all your answers to be no more than two minutes at the most, but many should be far shorter of course. At the other extreme – as we've already seen – try to avoid one-word answers unless your interviewer is clearly asking for clarification only (for example, 'So you're 18 now or 19?').

■ *Use examples.* Give plenty of specific examples of your achievements, challenges and successes. Be prepared to back up every assertion, and demonstrate every skill or achievement, with a concrete example.

■ *Remember the job description.* Keep your answers specific to the job in question. If your interviewer asks you, for example, what your greatest strength is, pick one which will be important in this job – and give an example of it.

■ *Pause if you need to.* If you want to think for a moment before you start answering a question, that's fine. It shows you're considering it carefully.

■ *Don't lie.* Be as honest as you can in your answers. You can – and should – put a positive spin on the truth, but don't change the facts. This includes admitting if you don't know the answer to a question, rather than floundering.

■ *Don't criticize your present employer.* If you're new to the job market, don't denigrate your tutor or your college course. It can make you look negative and picky (the interviewer may wonder what the other side of the story is), and it will certainly make your interviewer question your loyalty.

■ *Don't give away your current employer's secrets.* If you are being interviewed by one of your current employer's competitors, they may try to get you to say more than you should about your current employer's plans and organization. Just remember that much as they may want this information, they are also testing you. If you'll give away your present employer's secrets to a competitor, how loyal will you be to them if they give you the job?

## what the experts say

You'll be interested to know what the experts consider the key dos and don'ts of handling interviews. So here is a list of top points from Career World (a leading career management and outplacement consultancy).

*Do:*

■ Answer the question that is asked and do not volunteer irrelevant information.

■ Keep your answers concise and concentrate on the facts, not opinions.

■ Speak clearly and confidently and do not allow yourself to be discouraged.

■ Constantly remind yourself that you have something to sell and focus on how you can make a positive contribution in the role.

*Don't:*

■ Try to be too clever.

■ Lie, pretend or give evasive answers.

■ Lose your temper, get flustered, panic.

■ Criticize your former employers.

# Types of questions

As well as the specific questions covered in the next couple of chapters, there are general types of questions you need to be prepared for. Here's a quick rundown:

- *Hypothetical questions.* These ask, 'If $x$ happened, what would you do?' The thing to recognize is that there isn't necessarily a right answer. The interviewer may be more interested in how you go about addressing the problem than in your final outcome. It's fine to pause and think for a moment before you answer.

- *Technical questions.* If you are being interviewed for a technical post, be ready for questions which ask you to take the interviewer through a problem or process. This may be a hypothetical situation they set, or they may ask you to give an example from your own experience and take them through it in detail. So be ready for this kind of question, with examples prepared.

- *Stress questions.* Some interviewers will deliberately try to rile you or put you under pressure as a test. They want to see how you respond to this treatment. Many people feel this kind of interviewing technique is ethically dubious, and even question whether they want to work for someone who uses this tactic. But if you still want the job – and you may well feel that for the post you're applying for this interview method is justified – you'd better make sure you remain calm and pleasant no matter what the pressure.

---

**Just imagine...**

... the interviewer suddenly rounds on you and accuses you of lying about your qualifications. You become indignant and defensive. Only later does it dawn on you that they never really doubted your qualifications. They just wanted to know if you would stay calm and unflustered under pressure.

**Whoops...**

# Different types of interview

You will often find yourself in a one-to-one interview, very probably with the person who will be your line manager if you get the job. But of course, that's not the only type of interview there is. Almost all the guidelines in this book apply to any kind of interview, but there are a few extra pointers worth considering if you find yourself in one of the other types of interview.

## Panel interview

You may find yourself interviewed by three or four people. This might include the line manager for the job, someone from personnel, perhaps a technical person if it is a technical post, maybe a union representative, perhaps even a psychologist.

Panel interviews tend, by their nature, to be more formal than some one-to-one interviews. This can make them more stressful, but there's no reason why they should be any harder to handle than any other interview. You should know in advance that you will be interviewed by a panel. Try to find out their names – if you didn't realize you'd be seeing a panel until your arrival, ask the receptionist for their names. Write them down.

Bear in mind that HR professionals and line managers have different approaches to interviews. HR people conduct interviews for a living, they do lots of it and they know exactly what they are looking for. They won't have to work directly with you so their concerns are fairly black and white: they want you to match their employee specification as closely as possible.

The line manager, by contrast, may hate doing interviews for all you know, and will appreciate all the help you can give them, so be chatty and interested. They will also be wondering whether you'd have a good working relationship with them and with the rest of the team, so let them see that you're easy to get along with. So, know who is who and suit your answers most specifically to the person who has asked the question, while taking account of the rest of the panel too.

**Did you know?**

Panel interviews are particularly popular in the public sector. So if you're applying for a public sector job, ask if you'll be interviewed by a panel. If the answer's yes, you can get their names and job titles in advance. Memorize them, so you can address them by name in the interview (don't overdo this – show you've done your homework but don't keep using their names or you start to sound insincere).

Just remember:

- Shake hands with everyone on the panel. If it happens to be a large panel – more than about half a dozen – your alternative is to make a spot decision as you walk in that you will shake hands only with the chairperson (the one who stands and greets you), unless the others offer you a hand.

- Make eye contact with everyone on the panel, and make sure they all feel included in your answers.

- Give the bulk of your attention to the person who asked the question you arc answering.

- When you come to ask questions of your own, direct them primarily at the person who is chairing the interview (it'll be obvious who this is).

## Sequential interview

This is more common in larger organizations. You may find yourself in a series of one-to-one interviews with different people – maybe the line manager for the job, a more senior manager, a personnel representative, perhaps a technical person. Apart from the danger of feeling you're running a mental marathon, this is quite a good system for you. You get to start each interview afresh, so even if you feel you underperformed at the last one, you can still give a stunning performance at the next.

The interviewers, of course, are not operating in isolation. They will have discussed in advance what areas each will cover, and they will compare notes at the end before reaching a decision. They may also chat to each other between interviews. If this happens, you may find yourself being questioned about something you've already covered with the previous interviewer – very possibly they have asked the next person to probe the same area.

With sequential interviews, you need to bear in mind that each interviewer is looking at a different aspect of your application. There's no point in them all repeating the same exercise with you, after all.

---

### Pairing up

See if you can match up the following questions with the person most likely to ask them, bearing in mind that different interviewers have different areas of interest and expertise.

**A** Personnel manager

**1** What do you see as your greatest strength?

**B** Line manager

**2** Where do you see yourself in five years' time?

**C** Technical manager

**3** What sort of team player are you?

**D** Senior manager

**4** How would you respond to a software failure on the ZP21?

Answers:    A3; B1; C4; D2

---

I can't swear that you will never be asked each of these questions by one of the other interviewers than the one indicated. But the point here is that you need to be aware of what each interviewer is looking for, and give answers and examples which relate your ability to do the job to their particular discipline.

## Telephone interview

Some interviewers use telephone interviews as a quick way of slimming down a lengthy list of applicants into a shortlist for interview. Others may use them if the job involves a lot of telephone work, so they can assess your telephone and communication skills. They are also often used as an initial interview for overseas jobs. The interviewer may arrange an appointment for a telephone interview with you, or they may not. You won't necessarily get any warning that they are trying to contact you – the first you hear of it may be the phone call.

So if there's any chance of a phone call from the interviewer – for example if you're applying for a job which entails spending a lot of time on the telephone – you need to be ready for it:

- Keep a copy of the CV and the application form by the phone, along with a pen and paper.

- Keep your diary near the phone – if they like the sound of you on the phone they may arrange an interview.

- If you may be out when they call, make provision for this. Give best times to contact you on your CV or covering letter, consider getting an answerphone if you don't already have one, and brief anyone else who may answer your phone to take clear messages with names, phone numbers and so on.

- Treat the interview with the same importance you would a face-to-face interview. It may feel less formal, but it matters just as much.

- If you are not alone in the house, do your best to arrange to take the call in private. It's fine to ask the interviewer to hold on while you pick up another extension.

- Sit down during the interview if you can, remember to use the right body language (it will affect your tone of voice), and smile readily even though no one can see you.

- Make sure you write down the name of the interviewer and any other details they give you, such as their phone number, or directions on how to find them if they invite you for interview.

**Selection savvy**

If you're offered a face-to-face interview at the end of a phone interview, take down the details. Then write confirming the interview arrangements. It all goes to give the interviewer a great impression of your efficiency and professionalism.

# Making an exit

The interviewer will signal when the interview is over. And just like any good salesperson, you may not expect to clinch a deal on the spot, but you will at least want to agree the next step. So ask what happens next, and when. You want to know whether there'll be a second round of interviews, whether you'll hear by phone or by letter, when they'll be in touch, and so on.

Apart from that, when the interview ends, stand up, collect your things and leave promptly. Before you go, shake hands with the interviewer again if they offer you a hand. Thank them for seeing you, smile warmly (however you feel inside) and make a clean exit.

If the interviewer accompanies you to reception or to the main exit, chatting as you go, remember that you are still on show. Don't be lulled by the official end to the interview into making any unguarded comments.

## A thoroughly professional approach

Adopt a professional tone and style throughout the interview:

- Speak clearly.
- Don't ask too many questions until you are invited to.
- As far as the tone of the interview goes, take your lead from the interviewer.
- Don't ask about salary.

When it comes to answering questions:

- Don't ramble.
- Use examples.
- Fit your responses to the specific requirements of the job.
- Pause before you answer if you need to.
- Don't lie.
- Don't criticize your present employer.

Be ready for particular types of questions, such as hypothetical questions, so you can give the kind of answer the interviewer is looking for. And if your interview is not one to one, bear in mind the guidelines for other types of interview.

# 7 The most popular interview questions

There are some questions you can expect to be asked at most interviews, so these are the ones you should really be prepared for. There are certain things an interviewer is bound to want to know about you, and these are reflected in these questions. They will often come in the first half of the interview, since they are generally questions that the interviewer will be asking all the candidates.

We're about to go through a list of popular interview questions, so you can see the best kind of answer to give to each one. But of course, there are some general guidelines which apply to every answer you give. So let's look at these first. We've already gone through the key points in terms of your style of answering in the last chapter; now let's look a bit more closely at the content. The key things to remember when you answer any question are:

- *Keep your answer relevant.* If you are asked to outline your strengths, don't give a long list. Pick one or two key areas. You may have a dozen strengths, but just pick the ones which your interviewer most needs the successful candidate for this job to have.

- *Listen to the question, and answer the question you've been asked.* Don't sidestep difficult questions. Your interviewer isn't stupid – they'll notice you're doing it and they won't like it.

- *And answer **only** the question you are asked;* don't give lots of extraneous information. Keep your answers as brief as you can without omitting anything relevant.

> When asked what impresses them least in a candidate, most professional inter-
> viewers cited 'not listening to the question' as a major factor. This includes
> answering the question the candidate wants to answer, rather than the one they
> were actually asked.

# The most popular questions

The next chapter is about tough interview questions. You might think
that some of these ones here are tough; that's because the most popular questions are in this chapter, including those which could have
qualified for inclusion in the next chapter.

The answers recommended here are not a script; the idea is to let
you know the kind of answer that will impress the interviewer. You
will need to put it in your own words, and find your own examples to
give.

## Tell me about yourself

This is not an invitation to give your life history. In fact, you really need
the interviewer to be more specific before you can give the answer they
want. So ask them, 'What aspect of myself would you like me to tell
you about?' They are most likely to ask you to talk about what you're
like at work.

You should aim to describe the kind of person you are in a couple of
minutes at most. Concentrate on positive qualities, and link them to
the key responsibilities of the job you're applying for. For example:
'I'm a people person – I enjoy working with people and being part of a
team. I'm the sort of person who likes to get stuck into a project, and
I really enjoy seeing a project right through from initial planning to the
final stages …', and so on.

Should they ask to hear about what you're like away from work,
you still want to give them an answer which means you're cut out for
the job on offer. So again, if you want to show you're a good team
player, you might tell them, 'I'm very social; I have lots of friends

and I spend a lot of time with them. I play a lot of sports such as ice hockey.'

I'm not suggesting here that you lie. You've got plenty of time to think about this question before you get to the interview and be ready with suitable and honest answers about your personal or business life. If the job calls for a good team player, for example, it's likely you are one or you wouldn't be applying, so you probably have plenty of examples you could choose from.

### 5 phrases that employers love to hear

1 'Tell me more about the organization.' The interviewer wants to know that you are interested in the company itself, and not just what it can do for you.

2 'What would my promotion prospects be in this job?' This shows that you are ambitious and eager to do well – both positive attributes.

3 'I really enjoy a challenge.' Again, this shows enthusiasm for the job, even when it's not all going smoothly.

4 'I notice that the trend in this industry is…' You've really done your research here, and taken an interest in the wider context beyond the job on offer and even the organization.

5 'Can I give you an example…?' The more you can illustrate your answers to the questions with anecdotes and examples from your past experience, the better picture of you the interviewer will be able to form. This is exactly what they want to hear.

## What do you enjoy most in your current job?

This can be a kind of trick question. The interviewer is tempting you to indicate that there are things you don't like about your job. If that's so, presumably there will be things about this job that you don't like too – which isn't very encouraging. So the only answer you can really give is to say that you enjoy everything about your job.

If you think this sounds a little implausible, you can pick out one or two especial favourite parts of the job – making sure that they will be important parts of this job too, should you get it. So you might say, 'I'm lucky, really. I can't think of anything I don't enjoy about my job. But I suppose the thing I enjoy most is dealing directly with customers. That's why I've applied for this job; because I'd like the opportunity to spend even more of my time doing it.'

This answers the other obvious flaw in the 'I enjoy everything' answer, which is that it begs the question, 'Why are you looking for another post?'

### what the experts say

When asked how they would advise candidates to answer questions, interviewers' answers included:

- Keep to the point.
- Always use examples to back up your answers.
- Once you've finished your answer, stop talking.

## What is the biggest challenge you've faced at work?

So long as you're prepared, this is a great question. You need to have an answer ready for it in order to get the best from it. The idea is that you not only describe the challenge, but also how you coped with it. So you need to pick an example which leaves you looking good.

There is something else behind this question too: the interviewer is also finding out what you consider a challenge. So think hard about the example you want to pick. Will it be a tough decision? A difficult situation? A system that needed overhauling to improve results? You get to choose, so pick something which will be relevant to this job, as always.

Just one rule of thumb to follow: it's dangerous to pick an example that involves problems with other people. It can give the impression that you find getting on with others is a big challenge.

## Selection savvy

Although you need to prepare your answers in advance, it's not a good idea to learn them by rote. You'll sound as if you're giving a stilted recitation. Just prepare the key points you want to make.

## Why do you want to leave your present job?

It doesn't matter if the real reason is that you can't stand working with your boss any longer, or the company pays pathetically low salaries. Keep that to yourself. The interviewer is looking for a positive reason for moving forward, not a negative aim to avoid a job you're not happy in.

The only really good answer to this question is, 'Because I want to broaden my experience and I think I can do that better in a new organization' (or words to that effect). If it's relevant to the job you can expand on this briefly. For example, if the job entails giving a lot of presentations you might say, 'In particular, I enjoy presenting and it's something I've become very good at. Unfortunately, there aren't that many opportunities for me to develop my skills further where I am now.'

## Just imagine...

... you are being interviewed by someone friendly and sympathetic, who asks you why you're looking for another job. You decide to be completely honest, so you tell them it's because you were passed over for a promotion you're convinced you deserve, and now you have to work under the person who got the job in your place, and who isn't half as experienced as you. Your interviewer smiles sympathetically, and imagines exactly the same situation arising if they offered you the job.

**Whoops...**

## What is your present (or most recent) boss like?

Never criticize any of your bosses – current, recent or otherwise. The interviewer may be your future boss, and wants to hear you being loyal to other bosses even behind their backs. So always be positive – even if your boss is a first rate sh**. Just say something like, 'I'm lucky to have a boss who is very good at her job', and leave it there.

The point is not only that your interviewer wants to see that you are loyal, but also that your interviewer is aware they don't know the other side of the story. So *you* may know your complaints are justified, but to your interviewer they may just make you sound like a carping whinger who is likely to talk about them in the same terms if they employ you.

■■■ what the experts say ■■■■■■■■■■■■■■■■■■■■■■■■

Here's a handy piece of advice from Phil Boyle, MD of Ramsey Hall (an executive recruitment company): 'Rephrase the question as the early part of the answer. This will give the interviewer the opportunity of correcting the question if you have misunderstood it.'

## What do you think is the role of a ... (whatever your current job is)?

You should have thought this question through before you are asked it (as you should all the questions in this chapter). I can't tell you the answer, since I don't know what post you've applied for. But you need to answer in terms of the big picture:

■ the overall objective of the job
■ key responsibilities.

As you may realise, you can pick up big clues from the job description if you're applying for a job in your usual line of work. But you will also want to draw on your own experience.

This question is sometimes given as a test; if this happens the interviewer will interrupt to disagree with you. Their aim is to see whether you can defend your case calmly and convincingly, so don't be thrown by their interruption. Ask them politely to justify their assertion that your description of the role is wrong ('What makes you say that?'). Then show that you can argue your case well and without becoming defensive.

## What do you know about our company?

This is a great opportunity to demonstrate that you've done your homework. Keep to the relevant points – size, turnover, nature of the business, growth and business ethos (for example, 'I know you're a young, growing organization with a reputation for developing people'). Keep it brief, but add one or two things that suggest you've gone deeper than merely reading the annual report. For example: '… and I notice in the trade press that you've just signed a couple of very big deals in eastern Europe.'

### Selection savvy

If you're a graduate applying for your first job, your interviewer will want to know about your university career, and how it has helped to make you suitable for this job. From what subject you read to what your extra-curricular interests were, you can expect to answer questions on the following topics:

■ Why you chose your particular course.

■ How your studies relate to this job.

■ What project work you've done.

■ What extra-curricular activities you got involved in.

## Why do you want this job?

Try not to waffle about challenges and prospects. Talk in terms of benefits to them, and be specific about the kind of challenge you enjoy. For example: 'I'm a great organizer, and I'm looking for a post which gives me scope to plan and organize', or 'I get great satisfaction from working in a successful team, and this job seems to call for someone who can fit well into a tight, well-motivated team'.

This is also a good opportunity to show off the research you've done into the company – again keeping it brief and relevant. So you might say something like, 'I find growing companies have a more exciting, dynamic atmosphere to work in, and I know you've been growing by an average of six per cent for the last four years.'

## What do you feel you can bring to this job?

This is another question which gives you a chance to shine. You need to link your past experience or skills to the requirements of the job. So pick about three key strong points in your favour which are relevant to this job. For example: 'I'm very experienced at dealing with customers, including tricky ones. I get on easily with other people so I work well in a team. And I'm naturally organized and find it easy to handle paperwork and fit in with whatever systems I need to. As I understand it, these are all important skills for this job.'

## How long would you expect to stay with this company?

The interviewer isn't going to employ someone who'll be off again before they've got their full value from them. So indicate that you'd like to stay a few years. 'I'd like to settle with this company and grow and develop within it. I see myself staying as long as I keep progressing here and making a contribution.'

**Selection savvy**

Be prepared for the interviewer to ask you questions in a different form from the one given here, or prepared in your mind. They may ask you, 'What experience do you have of dealing with difficult customers?' Equally, they may try to elicit the same information by asking, 'Tell me about a difficult customer you've had to deal with. What did you do?' Or even, 'What do you think is the key to dealing with tricky or angry customers?' All of these are essentially different forms of the same question – you will need to be able to recognize them all as being a cue for the answer you've prepared.

## What are your greatest strengths?

Go for it. This is a perfect question – just focus your answers on the key responsibilities of the job to make sure your strengths are relevant to your interviewer. And make sure you don't waffle on for too long; pick one or two key strengths which are really important for this job.

## What is your biggest weakness?

Oooh, tricky. This is one of those questions which also belongs in the next chapter really – it's a toughie. It invites you to say something negative about yourself. Resist. The best defence to use is one of the following:

- humour ('Double choc-chip ice cream')
- something personal, not work related ('I'm useless at getting round to household jobs – changing lightbulbs and fixing leaky taps')
- something from long ago, which you have now learnt from ('Fifteen years ago I'd have said paperwork, but I've learnt to set aside half an hour at the start of every day for it. Now I reckon I'm more on top of the paperwork than the rest of my colleagues')

■ something which your interviewer will see as a strength ('I'm dreadful at stopping in the middle of something. I tend to stay at work until a task is done, even though my family often complain that I'm late home').

All of these questions should avoid giving away any real weaknesses (should you have any), and they also avoid making you come across as arrogant and too perfect – something which really gets up interviewers' noses.

## Where do you see yourself in five years' time?

You want to be careful how you answer this because, if you give a specific goal and the interviewer knows they cannot fulfil it, they will be put off hiring you. So keep it open. But remember that they want to know you have drive and will keep increasing your value to them. Say something like, 'I'm certainly ambitious, and I like to keep moving and progressing. But you can't fit a job to a preset list of conditions. I find it's far more rewarding to let the job lead you forward.'

## How would your colleagues describe you?

This is an invitation to list your strong points, so grab it. Concentrate on your plus points as a colleague – supportive, a good team player, and so on. As with all these questions, it's unwise to make any outrageous claims. You could well come unstuck if your references are checked out or when you start the job, if you're offered it. But of course you'll put the best complexion on things. So if you're a bit of a loner but get on with everyone, you might give an answer like, 'They'd say I was one of the quieter members of the team, popular and can be relied on to pull with the team when it's facing any kind of challenge'.

## How would your friends describe you?

'What friends?' is the wrong answer to this question. In fact, it runs along much the same lines as 'How would your colleagues describe you?' Don't be unrealistic about yourself, but pick out the strongest points which will be relevant. It's always worth mentioning loyalty and supportiveness.

The interviewer is simply trying to get a more rounded picture of the kind of person you are, to help them assess whether you'll fit in with the people you'll be working with.

## What outside interests do you have?

Your interviewer is trying to find out more about you. Your interests will tell them whether you are sporty, competitive, enjoy dangerous hobbies, like solo or group activities, and so on. Don't invent hobbies (you don't want your interviewer to say, 'Bungee jumping? Me too! Where's your favourite location round here for a jump? What kind of equipment do you use?'), but select those hobbies or interests which show you as the kind of person your interviewer is looking for.

## What have you read and enjoyed lately?

Don't make up some fashionable answer here, or name a leading business book you haven't actually read. You may be asked questions about your answer. You don't have to mention the most recent book you've read, so pick one you've genuinely enjoyed which is slightly offbeat – you're not one of the crowd. You might want to choose an unusual classic, an avant-garde title or a biography – pick something which will show a side of you you'd like the interviewer to see.

## Check you're ready

Here's a list of all the questions in this chapter. When you have prepared an answer to each one, jot down a note of it in the middle column. In the right-hand column, make a note of the best example you can give to back up your answer. Make sure you are ready to answer any of the questions in this chapter.

| Question | Answer | Example |
|---|---|---|
| Tell me about yourself. | | |
| What do you enjoy most in your current job? | | |
| What is the biggest challenge you've faced at work? | | |
| Why do you want to leave your present job? | | |
| What is your present (or most recent) boss like? | | |
| What do you think is the role of a … (whatever your current job is)? | | |
| What do you know about our company? | | |
| Why do you want this job? | | |
| What do you feel you can bring to this job? | | |
| How long would you expect to stay with this company? | | |
| What are your greatest strengths? | | |
| What is your biggest weakness? | | |
| Where do you see yourself in five years' time? | | |
| How would your colleagues describe you? | | |
| How would your friends describe you? | | |

| Question | Answer | Example |
|---|---|---|
| What outside interests do you have? | | |
| What have you read and enjoyed lately? | | |

---

### Ready answers

Be ready for the questions you are most likely to be asked, and make sure you:

- Listen to the question.

- Answer the question you've been asked.

- Be as brief as you can without omitting anything relevant.

- Put your answers in terms which show you are suitable for this particular job.

# 8 Tough interview questions

OK, I know that almost any question can seem tough. But compared with 'How long have you been in your current job?', these questions are *really* tough. They're not necessarily intended to make you wriggle (though some are); they may simply be the interviewer's best way of finding out what they need to know.

As far as the interviewer is concerned, this isn't a competition. You're both on the same side so there should be no element of trying to get the better of you, or knock you down a peg or two; certainly not if your interviewer is professional. Tough questions are generally tough simply because you're not sure how to answer them.

But the point is that, whatever the interviewer's intent, any of these questions might make you feel uncomfortable if you're not prepared for them. Well, that's OK. After this chapter you will be prepared.

### what the experts say

According to professional interviewers, they don't ask deliberately tough questions without a good reason. So what is a good reason? Chiefly:

- To see how you react under pressure.

- To confirm that you are telling the truth (if they doubt it).

Interviewers are particularly likely to see how you respond to questioning under pressure if they have some indication – for example, from psycho-metric tests – that you don't handle pressure as well as you might.

Whether or not the interviewer intends the question to be tough, you should still follow the same groundrules:

■ Stay calm.

■ Don't get defensive.

■ Pause for a moment before you answer if you wish.

The following questions are divided into broad categories to help you find your way around them:

■ questions about you

■ questions about your career

■ questions about this job

■ questions inviting you to criticize yourself

■ questions inviting you to be negative

■ questions about your salary

■ unexpected questions.

## Questions about you

Not all the questions in this section will necessarily apply to you. If you're applying for a job that doesn't involve working as part of a team, you're not likely to be asked about your teamwork skills. If you're not applying for a management job, you won't be asked about your management style. But whatever job you are being interviewed for, you'll find that some of the questions here will apply to you and you'll need to prepare answers.

## What will you be asked?

Have a look at the questions in this list, and think about which ones you're likely to be asked for each of the jobs listed. Tick those you think are most likely to be asked for each job.

|  | Production manager | Sales assistant | Accounts clerk | Project supervisor |
|---|---|---|---|---|
| 1. Are you a natural leader? | | | | |
| 2. What motivates you? | | | | |
| 3. How do you work in a team? | | | | |
| 4. How do you operate under stress? | | | | |
| 5. What do you dislike most at work? | | | | |
| 6. How well do you take direction? | | | | |
| 7. Do you enjoy routine tasks? | | | | |

## What motivates you?

You need to give an answer, as always, that also benefits your potential employer and links into the key responsibilities of the job. So don't say, 'My pay packet'. Give an answer such as, 'I'm happiest when I can see a project through from start to finish', or 'I get a real kick out of running a team that is happy and knows it is successful'.

## How well do you take direction?

Keep in mind the fact that your interviewer may well become your boss if this interview goes according to plan, so it's their direction you'll need to take. The answer, obviously, has to be that you take direction well. You can add credibility to your answer by expanding it to add something like, 'I don't see how a team can function effectively unless its members are happy to take direction from the team leader'.

## How do you handle criticism?

Again, your interviewer may be anticipating being your boss, and inevitably having to criticize you from time to time. They want to know whether the task will be easy for them, or whether you'll make it unpleasant.

So give an answer along the lines of: 'I'm happy to be given constructive criticism. In fact, I think being prepared to take constructive criticism on board is the only way I can hope to learn from mistakes and improve my performance.'

## Do you enjoy routine tasks?

You're not likely to be asked this question unless you're applying for a job which will entail routine tasks. So clearly your answer should be, 'Yes'. However, one-word answers aren't advisable, because your reply will carry more weight if you elaborate briefly to show that you understood the question and have thought out your response.

So you could add, 'Yes, I have an orderly approach to work and I get satisfaction from carrying out routine work successfully'.

## What is your management style?

There's no point in lying to questions like this, so give an honest answer. But again, make sure it's relevant. You don't need to give a 20-minute rant on the subject; just a couple of clear sentences will do: 'I prefer a carrot rather than a stick approach, and I have an open-door policy', or 'I believe a manager has to be firm with the team, and the team appreciate it so long as you are also scrupulously fair'. It helps to follow this with an anecdote – some example of a problem in your team which you resolved firmly but fairly, for example.

### Selection savvy

Never mention anything at interview that isn't on your CV. You may have managed to miss off those four months you spent stacking supermarket shelves without the gap showing on your CV. But if you make reference to it at the interview, it will call into question the credibility of your whole CV. So either put it on the CV, or make sure you don't refer to it at the interview.

## Are you a good manager?

This is a similar question to the one about your management style, but it is blunter. The answer clearly has to be 'Yes'; if you haven't already been asked about your style you can describe it briefly as we saw in the answer above. Again, it is also a good idea to relate a brief anecdote illustrating your approach to managing people.

## Are you a natural leader?

Since you're only going to be asked this if the job calls for a leader, the answer has to be affirmative. Follow your answer with one or two brief examples, bearing in mind that they don't have to come exclusively from work. You might point out that you were Head Boy or Girl at school, or that you direct your local amateur theatrical society, as well as giving an example from your work background.

Natural leaders, after all, often start young. So if you've been leading groups of people since you were at school, it suggests your leadership skills really are natural, and people follow you through choice.

## How do you work in a team?

This is another question you need to answer honestly, but pick a relevant way to express your teamwork style. Give a brief answer, such as, 'I enjoy being part of a team, and I like the flexibility it demands. I get a real kick out of collective success'. Follow your remarks with an anecdote or example demonstrating what you mean. If teamwork is an important part of the job, you should certainly expect this question (or a variant of it) and have an anecdote ready.

## How do you approach a typical project?

If you are applying for a project-based job, you should expect to be asked this question. You don't need to give a rambling answer, but show that you take into account the main components of effective project planning:

- Plan the schedule backwards from the completion/delivery date.
- Work out what you need to get the job done effectively and on time.
- Budget cost, time and resources.
- Allow a contingency.

## Best of three

It's a good idea to think of the three personal characteristics you most want to demonstrate to the interviewer. Any more than three, and your message will become diluted. So pick three characteristics (out of your numerous strong points) which:

- are genuinely strong traits of yours
- are important characteristics for the job you're applying for.

Once you have identified the three characteristics you want to promote, prepare examples and anecdotes which emphasize them, as well as making whatever other point you want to illustrate. And when asked questions such as, 'What would your boss say about you?', bring these characteristics directly into play.

Here is a list to give you an idea of the characteristics you could choose from (you may come up with others that aren't on this list):

- Honesty
- Drive
- Energy
- Flexibility
- Patience
- Confidence
- Good communication

- Enthusiasm
- Attention to detail
- Reliability
- Initiative
- Leadership
- Focus on objectives
- Good interpersonal skills

- Dedication
- Integrity
- Creativity
- Authority
- Diplomacy
- Determination
- Calmness under pressure

## How do you operate under stress?

Again, a question you'll only be asked if it applies to the job. A full answer will sell you better than a brief one. So say that you work well under pressure – say you enjoy it if that's true – and give an example of a time you've handled a situation well under pressure. You might also want to add that you practise good time management to make sure that you minimize the stress you have to operate under (but, as always, don't say this if it isn't true).

## How creative are you?

Again, a question for people who need to be creative. So, presumably, you have examples you can give; be ready with them. If you have to do a lot of creative thinking, outline one or two key creative techniques you use, too, to show that you take your creativity seriously.

## How do you get the best from people?

If you're a manager, this is a question you may well be asked. The kind of skills that interviewers want to hear about include:

- good communication
- teamwork skills
- recognizing each person as an individual
- setting a sound example
- praising good performances.

## How do you resolve conflict in your team?

You need to answer this question honestly, as always. And find an example of conflict in your team that you can use to demonstrate your skills at resolving it. The kind of techniques you need to demonstrate include:

- fairness
- addressing problems with individuals privately
- making sure you get to the root of the problem
- finding a solution that the people involved are willing to buy into.

Assuming it's true, you would also do well to point out, 'I find if a team is run fairly and the team members are well motivated, conflict very rarely arises.'

## Selection savvy

What do you do if you're faced with an incompetent interviewer? Well, the biggest mistake incompetent interviewers make – by one means or another – is that they don't encourage you to answer questions fully. They ask closed questions (requiring one-word answers), or they never ask you for examples or experiences to back up your claims.

The trick is to do their job for them. Volunteer full answers even if the questions don't demand them. Give examples without being asked. And if you have one of those interviewers who keeps wandering off the point, or stopping the interview to deal with interruptions, impress them by always being able to answer accurately when they ask, 'Where were we?'

## What would your boss say about you?

Your interviewer may well be your prospective boss, so be careful. They want to know that you're an effective worker, but they don't want you stepping on their toes. So describe yourself as any boss would want to see you. For example, 'My boss would describe me as hard working, easy to motivate and loyal. She'd say that I work well on my own initiative, and I'm a supportive member of the team.' Resist the temptation to say 'I *think* my boss would say ....'. Be positive and certain in your answer.

If your interviewer is likely to be approaching your present boss at some stage for a reference, make sure that your answer tallies with what your boss is likely to say about you when your interviewer puts this particular answer to the test.

## What do you dislike most at work?

You love work, remember? This interviewer can safely hire you, knowing that you will be well motivated every minute of your working life. So if asked, you can't think of anything you dislike. The only possible exception is if this job is very different from your last, in which case you might say something like, 'I really enjoy my work. But occasionally I get a little frustrated in a small company that I don't get to meet customers as often as I'd like. That's one of the reasons why this job appeals to me so much.'

### Selection savvy

Honesty is the best policy for several reasons:

- A skilled interviewer may well be able to tell if you're lying.

- Any dishonesty may show up when your interviewer checks references or qualifications, in which case they will certainly be put off you.

- If you successfully get the job by being dishonest, your new boss will notice as soon as you fail to live up to the working style or standards you 'promised' at interview. You may have got the job, but once you're in it you'll be off to a pretty poor start.

With intelligent handling of the questions, and following the guidelines here, you should be able to perform excellently at interview without any need to lie.

# Questions about your career

Your interviewer needs to know if you're at the right point on the career ladder for them. But they also need to know where you think you're going. Are you planning to move up the organization much faster or slower than they expect in this job? So the questions in this section are all designed to tell the interviewer how this job would fit into the broader picture for you in the long term.

This is one of those areas where it is important to be honest. It's not just that interviews can only work on the principle that everyone is honest, quite apart from the ethical approach to being honest. It's also the fact that if you mislead the interviewer, you could end up being offered a job which will be detrimental to your career. The interviewer knows far better than you whether this job suits your long-term aims – but only if you tell them straight what those aims are.

At the same time, you want this job, so you will – always – put your answers in the best possible light. But you'll do it without misleading the interviewer.

## Why have you been so long with your present employer?

The answer to avoid is one that implies you were getting stale and should have moved earlier. Any answer which contradicts this unspoken worry on the interviewer's part is fine. For example, 'I've been there for several years, but in a variety of different roles', or 'The job was growing constantly, so it felt as though I was undergoing frequent changes without actually changing employer'.

## Why have you been such a short time with your present employer?

Your interviewer doesn't want to take on someone who is going to leave in six months' time. So show them that you're not really a job-hopper, whatever your CV may appear to show. 'I'd like to settle in one company for several years, but I've found up until now that I've had to move in order to widen my experience and avoid getting stale in the job.'

## You look like a job-hopper to me

This is the previous question but worse. If it is not only your current or most recent employer that you've spent a short time with, but previous employers too, your interviewer will quite understandably be concerned that you'll leave them within a few months too. Nowadays people typically change jobs roughly every two to five years, but much more frequently than this looks worrying to a potential employer. And some industries expect their people to stay with them longer than that.

If your CV gives the impression that you barely sit down at your desk before you're off again, you can expect this question. So how do you reassure the interviewer that this time, you'd be here to stay? The last thing you want to do is launch into a lengthy, defensive justification for each job move in turn. Far better to give a catch-all reason for moving so frequently.

So adopt this kind of approach: 'I'd like to find a company I can settle down in and really make a mark. Until now I've found that I've had to change jobs in order to keep finding challenge in my work. For example …' Then you can briefly explain just one of your career moves, and why it made so much sense. Finish by saying, 'What I'm looking for is a company dynamic enough for me to find fresh challenges without having to move to another organization.'

## Why haven't you found a new job yet?

The implication behind this question is that you can't be much good if no one wants to give you a job. So you need to indicate that it has been your choice to spend some time job-hunting. You need to give a reply such as, 'It's important that I only accept a job that seems really right for me, and where I can see that I can make a contribution to the company'.

If you have turned down any offers, say so: 'I have had job offers, but I didn't feel the positions were right for me, and that I was right for the companies concerned.'

## What were your most significant achievements in your current (or most recent) job?

It's unlikely that this job will require exactly the same achievements as the last – although it's great if you can find a clear parallel. So what the interviewer really wants to know about is the qualities you must have exhibited in order to score the achievement. Be ready with something which is:

- recent (or the implication is you've achieved little of note since)
- difficult to achieve
- as relevant as possible to the job you're applying for.

### Selection savvy

Many people feel uncomfortable blowing their own trumpet, which is precisely what you need to do at interview. However, you do want to avoid appearing arrogant, so being too cocky is a legitimate worry. There is a tendency to compensate for this by prefixing remarks with phrases such as 'I feel' or 'I think', as in:

- 'I think I'm a good manager.'
- 'I feel my strongest points are …'
- 'I think my greatest achievement in my current job has been …'

While this may solve the problem of not appearing too arrogant, it creates another problem: it weakens and dilutes whatever you say after it. You're not saying, for example, that you *are* a good manager – merely that you *think* you are. You can get round this by substituting a stronger phrase in place of 'I think'. For example:

- 'I believe I'm a good manager.'
- 'I would say my strongest points are …'
- 'Colleagues tell me my greatest achievement has been …'

## If you could start again, what career decisions would you make differently?

You're on a hiding to nothing if you start trying to think of hypothetical improvements to your past career. Anything you say will suggest that you're not happy with the way things are – and why would anyone want to hire someone who doesn't really want to be where they are?

So the only reasonable answer is that you wouldn't change anything; you're happy with things as they are now. You might add something like, 'I'm not the kind of person to look back with regrets. I like to invest my energy in looking forward.'

## Do you consider your career so far has been successful?

Clearly it's better to be a success than a failure, so unless you've spent long periods out of work and stuck in dead-end jobs, the answer to this question is 'Yes'. To expand on this answer (as you always should on a one-word answer), you can go on to define success in your own terms. This is particularly sensible if your career on paper may look less than outstanding, even if it's respectable.

Perhaps you haven't moved up the career ladder as fast as you might. So you might say, 'What matters to me – more than money or status – is to have a job which is interesting and challenging, and I've been lucky in that respect. So my career so far has been very successful.'

And what if your career has had its low points, and perhaps not brought you as far as it might? There's no point in pretending your CV glitters when it clearly doesn't – so show you are positive and looking ahead: 'I've had one or two career problems in the past, but those are firmly behind me. From now on I intend to build on the good breaks I've had and enjoy a very successful career.'

## When would you expect promotion?

Don't give a firm timescale here. The answer is, you should expect promotion when you deserve it. 'I would hope to be promoted once I have demonstrated my value to the company, and shown that I'm worth it.'

And show how this job suits your long-term aims: 'That's why I want to join a company that is growing so that the promotion opportunities will be there when I'm ready to move up', or 'That's why I want to join a large organization so there are plenty of opportunities when I've gained the skills and experience'.

## Selection savvy

Certain questions are technically illegal, or can be if there isn't a sound, relevant reason for asking them. These include questions relating to your race, religion or sex, questions about your medical history, or about your future plans for a family, and that sort of thing. But what do you do if you're asked? You can obviously answer if you wish to, but what if you'd rather not?

While you're perfectly entitled to get defensive and demand that your interviewer retract the question, such behaviour may not help you get this job. Your best bet is to say politely, 'Can I ask why you need to know that?' Unless there's a legitimate reason, this will almost certainly lead to a retraction. If they persist in asking you something totally unreasonable, you will have to choose between refusing firmly or answering anyway (whether truthfully or not).

# Questions about this job

Your interviewer is well aware that there are thousands of jobs being advertised every day. So why have you applied for this particular one? They are looking for evidence that the job really suits you – that it fits in with your general aptitudes, suits your long-term goals, and involves doing things you enjoy.

This is why they will use these questions to delve deeper into how strongly you feel about this job, how enthusiastic you really are about it, and how much you really think you would enjoy it and be able to contribute to the organization.

## How can you attend this interview while you're employed elsewhere?

The hidden pitfall here is that you must avoid coming across as being dishonest in any way. So if you told your boss you had to stay home for the washing machine maintenance engineer to call, or that you had a doctor's appointment, keep quiet about it. Otherwise your interviewer knows that if they offer you the job, they'll be wondering what's going on every time you ask for time off to go to the doctor.

Ideally, your boss knows you're looking for work and is aware you're at an interview. However, this isn't often the case. Assuming your boss actually has no idea where you are, the only valid justification for taking time off to come here is that you were owed holiday or time off and you took it in order to be at this interview.

## How does this job fit into your career plan?

It's dangerous to commit yourself too precisely to a career plan. So you might say something like, 'Business changes so rapidly these days, it's hard to plan precisely. But I know I want to get ahead in this industry/in marketing/in management and I think the opportunities to do that in this company are excellent.'

## What appeals to you least about this job?

Careful here. Naming almost anything will give the interviewer the impression that you are less than 100 per cent enthusiastic about this job. So either tell them that it all appeals to you or, if you feel too glib giving this kind of answer, come up with a part of the job which is:

- a small part of it
- of no major importance
- universally unpopular.

One of the best examples of this is filing, or paperwork in a job where the paperwork isn't a significant part of the job (but absolutely not if it's important to the job). But you should still express it in positive terms: 'I can't say I find paperwork terribly inspiring. But it's important to make sure it gets done. And actually, it can be quite therapeutic.'

## Just imagine...

You're asked what appeals least about the job. You laugh and say 'Probably having to be here by 8.30 in the morning.' You meant it flippantly and the interviewer shares the joke with you, but privately thinks that sort of remark doesn't come from nowhere. If they offer you the job, they wonder, will you get fed up with it because of the early starts? Will you have a time-keeping problem? Will it take you ages to get going once you arrive in the mornings ...?

**Whoops...**

## Are you talking to other organizations as well as us?

You want to show your interviewer that you're in demand. It makes you a more attractive prospect, and if you're offered the job it can help to push up the salary you manage to negotiate. At the same time, if you tell them you've had three other offers already, they may be put off you if they still have a long way to go – another round of interviews, for example. So indicate that you are talking to others without suggesting you're on the verge of taking another job. If it's not a downright lie, let them know if you're doing well. For example, 'I've reached the final round of interviews with three other organizations.'

## What other types of job or organization are you applying to?

There's no need to divulge exactly who you've applied to. Occasionally you may be asked directly where else you've applied, but you can avoid answering by saying that the companies concerned haven't advertised and you don't feel you should divulge the information. That lets you off the hook and shows you can keep a confidence.

But the interviewer can get round it with this question – asking not for names of companies but merely types of job and company. The important thing here is to show that you want this job. If it becomes plain that you're applying for all sorts of different jobs in different industries, it rather casts doubt on your commitment to this post. So indicate that you're applying for similar jobs within the same field.

## How long would it take you to make a useful contribution to this company?

You might be thinking that you can't answer this question without more information. Quite right. So ask for the information you need:

- What would my key objectives be for the first six months?
- Are there any specific projects you would need me to start work on straight away?

You can use the answers to these enquiries to help with your answer. But broadly speaking, you should indicate that (unless there is an urgent project) you would expect to spend the first week or two settling in and learning the ropes. After that you'd expect to be making a useful contribution within the first few weeks, and to show significant successes within four to six months.

## You may be overqualified for this job

The worry the interviewer is revealing here is that if they offer the job you will quickly become bored and leave. You may have reservations on this front yourself, but at this stage you should still be doing your best to get the job. If you're going to turn it down, do it when it's offered – don't write it off half-way through the interview.

So for the moment, you're going to give the best answer you can. Say that strong, dynamic companies can always use whatever talents they have to hand. You want to stay with the company for a while and, if your experience and skills are strong enough, you're sure they will find a way to keep you challenged and making a full contribution.

## What do you think are the key trends in this industry?

This question isn't difficult so long as you've done your research – which is what the interviewer wants to establish. This question is really the advanced version of, 'What do you know about our company?'. So the important thing here is to make sure you do your homework, and identify the key industry trends, ready to impress your interviewer.

Even if you're applying for a job in the industry you already work in, you should still prepare an answer to this question. It won't necessarily come to you, clearly and succinctly, in the heat of the moment.

### Selection savvy

One of the ways in which interviewers can test you is by asking you more than one question at a time. For example: 'How would you approach a typical project, what is the biggest project you have handled in the past, and what were the major difficulties you encountered?'

Unskilled interviewers may do this unintentionally, but skilled interviewers are more likely to do it as a test of your intelligence. The more of the questions you answer (and you have to hold each one in your head while you answer the others), the brighter they will assume you are. If you repeat the question back to them as soon as they ask it, this will help you to fix it in your mind.

# Questions inviting you to criticize yourself

Uh-oh. These are tricky questions, and ones you want to be careful with. You have a bit of a dilemma here: you don't want to admit to any faults or errors but, on the other hand, arrogance is one of the factors most interviewers cite as being particularly irritating. So how can you avoid conceding mistakes without appearing cocky and just too perfect?

One of the classic questions in this category is 'What is your biggest weakness?' – a question so popular we dealt with it in the last chapter.

And the recommended type of answer we looked at then applies for all these questions too. Here are the four techniques for criticizing yourself without admitting to anything damaging:

- Use humour – but be careful. This isn't the best approach if you sense that your interviewer has no sense of humour. But if they seem ready for a laugh, and it suits your personality to do it, you can use humour. If you do it every time, however, it starts to look like a cop-out (which it is, of course).

- Give an example from your personal rather than your work life, where the question allows. For example, 'I used to find getting up in the mornings a real challenge, but since I started walking the dog before breakfast I find I really enjoy getting up.'

- Pick something from a long time ago, which you can demonstrate that you've learnt from. For example, 'Decisions without a deadline used to be a problem for me – I never got round to making them. Then I discovered the trick of imposing a deadline on myself just so the decision would get made. Now I never delay decisions unnecessarily.'

- Give an answer which you claim is a fault or a weakness, but your interviewer will see as a strength. For example, 'I can be a bit of a perfectionist. I just can't bring myself to turn out work that I feel isn't as good as it could be.'

---

## 5 phrases that employers hate to hear

1 'Sorry I'm late.'

2 'I don't really know.' Unless the question is a factual one, employers want to hear you being positive and enthusiastic about answering questions.

3 'I don't get on with my boss' Maybe you don't, but the interviewer wants to hear that you are loyal publicly, regardless of your private feelings. That's a quality they're going to want in whoever they give this job to.

4 'What salary are you offering for this post?' This question suggests that you care only about what the organization can do for you, not about what you can do for it. The same goes for questions about hours of work and all the rest. (Time enough to discuss that after they offer you the job.)

5 'You're wrong...' or any other form of overt disagreement. If you get flustered or riled into speaking aggressively, it doesn't say much for your people skills. It's quite possible to disagree politely. Remember, the interviewer may be testing you to see how you respond.

## Describe a difficult situation which, with hindsight, you could have handled better

Again, the trick here is to be ready with something from a long time ago. And try to prepare an example where it really wasn't your fault you handled it as you did. For example, 'With hindsight, I can see that it would have been quicker to evacuate everyone straight down the main staircase rather than use the fire escape, but because the phones were down I had no way of knowing that the main staircase was safe.'

## What sort of decisions do you find difficult?

You've never found a decision difficult in your life, of course. But the danger with some of these questions is that if you come across as being too implausibly perfect, you risk sounding glib and arrogant. So you have to admit to some minor failings, but make sure they have been overcome or are irrelevant to the job you're applying for – or else make you sound human. So you could say, 'The kind of decisions I dislike most are the ones which other people won't like. They aren't actually difficult, but I don't like making a decision to sack someone, for example.' If you've never had to sack anyone, find another example of something others don't like.

## Describe a situation in which your work was criticized

If you pick an instance where the criticism was clearly unfair and you were in the right, you risk looking as if you are simply taking an opportunity to air an old grievance – maybe you're someone who bears grudges (the interviewer will think). So you need to go for the 'distant past' option.

Interviewers may well ask you this question – or a variation on it – if they want to see how you cope with tough questioning. So make sure you have an answer ready in case you need it. You should answer in two stages:

- Briefly describe the task and the criticism you received for it.
- Explain how you learnt from it and you haven't repeated such mistakes since.

Not only does this make you sound human, and as though you haven't been criticized for a long time, but it also shows that you can take constructive criticism on board and learn from it.

### Selection savvy

Whatever the temptation, don't argue with your interviewer. If they see you as difficult and argumentative it will put them off employing you. They may even be testing you to see how you respond to their belligerent questioning. So if you tell them you run a team of three people and they say, 'That's hardly managing, is it? This job entails running a team of ten', don't get defensive. Say something like, 'I can see that it looks very different on the surface, but I'd say the same principles apply whether you manage one person or a hundred.'

# Questions inviting you to be negative

These questions are intended to find out if you are naturally negative or even bitchy when given the opportunity, or whether your natural instinct is to be positive. So whatever you do, don't take the bait. Refuse to be critical or negative about other people or organizations.

## What is your present boss's greatest weakness?

'Where do I start?' is not the right response to this question. In the last chapter we looked at the popular question, 'What is your present (or most recent) boss like?'. This is the tough version of the same question – it really invites you to land yourself in it. So don't fall for it, no matter how long a list of complaints you may privately have about your boss. Remember, this interviewer may one day be your boss. So tell them what they would like to hear about themselves.

Say something along the lines of: 'To be honest, I'm lucky to have a very supportive boss who is good at her job and very easy to work with.' Then look as if you're really trying to think of a weakness and add, 'I can't think of anything – if I did it could only be something so picky it wouldn't be worth mentioning.'

## How do you evaluate your present company?

It's a great company which has taught you a lot and given you lots of excellent opportunities. I don't care what you tell your mates, as far as the interviewer is concerned, that's your answer and you're sticking with it.

This reply may understandably be followed with the question, 'Then why do you want to leave your job?' We looked at how to answer this in the last chapter (see page 64).

## What sort of people do you find it difficult to work with?

As always, you need to resist criticizing other people. Don't be drawn into bitching about the PA in your department who's always trying to boss people around, or the programmer who is always moaning about their workload. Start by saying that you generally find most people are easy to work with, but if you had to pick a type you found difficult it would be people who don't pull their weight, and don't seem to care about the standard of their work.

## Preparation exercises

You're bound to be asked some pretty tough questions during your interview. We all have areas we might prefer not to be asked about, or topics we find tricky. Or maybe we just get nervous when we're put on the spot. So here are a few ideas to help you prepare for the trickiest questions:

- Sit down and think up the five or six questions you'd least like to be asked. Maybe you spent a long time in one job without promotion, and you don't want to come across as a low achiever. Or perhaps you find some people tricky to deal with and you don't want to answer too many questions about how you handle difficult people. Write down your list of 'hate' questions, and then work out answers to all of them.

- Ask a few of your friends or colleagues to fire tough questions at you. Maybe you could ask them to call you out of the blue once or twice in the next few days, and fire tough questions at you.

- Ask a few friends and colleagues to tell you the toughest questions they've ever been asked at interview, and then work out how you'd answer them.

# Questions about your salary

The general rule when it comes to questions about salary is to get them to name a figure rather than allow them to force the ball into your court. If you name a salary, you can bet you'll never get more than the figure you've named. So unless – or until – you have a very clear idea of exactly what they're expecting to pay you, don't commit yourself to a specific figure.

The following questions are intended to get you to name your price. The recommended answers are intended to sidestep the issue without causing offence or appearing unreasonable. Once you are offered the job, *then* you can negotiate – following the guidelines set out in Chapter 14.

**Just imagine...**

You're asked what salary you're expecting, so you reply with the figure you had in mind: 'Somewhere around £22,000.' You are subsequently offered the job, at a salary of £22,000 – which you can hardly argue with since you named the figure yourself. Once you start the job you discover that colleagues doing a similar job to you are all earning at least £25,000.

**Whoops...**

## What is your present salary?

You don't want to answer this. If you're offered the job, they'll try to get away with paying you as close as they can to your existing salary – at best it will hold the negotiating level down. Say something such as, 'I think salaries can be misleading, as it's really the whole remuneration package that counts. Of course, that's harder to quantify.' Then ask if you can return to the question later, once you get to a point where you need to talk about it in more detail (i.e. when they offer you the job).

## What salary are you expecting?

You don't want to answer this one either, because there's no chance of getting any more than you say now, and a good chance of scaring them off if you ask too much. So answer a question with a question: 'What salary would you expect to pay for this post?' or ask what salary range has been allocated. If they refuse to answer at this stage, you can reasonably do so too.

If they quote a salary and ask for your response, let them know you were thinking of something a little higher, but not out of their reach (assuming you'd agree to that yourself). If they suggest a range, quote them back a range which is higher but overlaps. So if they say £20–25,000 you might say you were thinking of £24–28,000. You're edging them up, but you're not putting them off.

## How much do you think you're worth?

All these salary questions are good news, essentially. Why would they bother to ask unless they were thinking of offering you the job? This particular question is really the previous one again with a nasty twist to it. It's just a matter of justifying what you're asking for – once you've played the previous game of making them go first.

You should already have an idea of the going rate for the job in the industry or the organization (especially if it's an internal job), so ask for a little more and explain that you've studied salary surveys and so on and, since your experience and skills are above average for the job, you believe you're worth above the average pay. By the way, you can expect the interviewer to respond by saying that the figure you name is too high – that's just part of the negotiating tactic. Don't let it dent your confidence.

### Selection savvy

Never drop your guard at an interview. Trained interviewers are very skilled at catching you off guard to see how you react. They may be friendly and relaxed and then suddenly fire a tough question at you, or they may follow a series of easy questions with a trick one, having lulled you into a false sense of security.

So treat every question as a fresh start, and never assume that this is an easy interview. Pause before answering if you need to, so you can't be rail-roaded into making any unguarded comments.

# Unexpected questions

Some interviewers like to catch you off guard, and many of these questions are intended for just that purpose. They're not just trying to be unpleasant for the sake of it. They either have a good reason for wanting to know the answer, or they want to know how you cope with the pressure of an unexpected question. The key rules here are:

- Pause before you answer if you need to (interviewers rather like this as they can see you're really thinking about your answer).

- If you're unsure what the interviewer means by the question, ask for clarification.

- Stay cool and unflustered, and don't argue with the interviewer.

## Sell me this pen

Some interviewers like asking this kind of question even if you're not applying for a sales post. The aim is to see that you focus not on features ('It's solid silver') but on the benefits to them ('It will impress people'). So give them four or five benefits of the pen (or notepad, or paperclip or whatever they've asked you to sell them), and then finish, half jokingly, with a standard closing technique: 'Shall I put you down for two dozen?' or 'Would you prefer it in black or red?'

## Tell me a story

This is a semi-trick question. You're supposed to demonstrate whether you have a sufficiently logical mental approach to ask for the question to be more specific before you answer it. So ask the interviewer, 'What kind of story?' They will probably ask for a story about you, and are likely to specify whether they want a work-related or a personal story. Then just relate some anecdote which shows you in a good light (so have one ready).

## What do you think about privatization/global warming/the Balkans (or whatever)?

The interviewer is trying to find out how much of an interest you take in the world in general, and also to get an idea of your values and attitude to life. Whatever the topic, you need to demonstrate in your answer that you can see both sides of an argument, that you don't view things in an over-simplistic way, that you can discuss a subject fluently and that you are capable of making judgements.

So don't rant on about your particular views (if you hold strong views) without acknowledging the other side of the debate. You are most likely to be asked these kinds of questions by companies to whom they are relevant. Pharmaceutical companies may ask your views on supplying cost-price drugs to developing countries; banks might ask your views on interest rates. So take into account their likely view on the subject.

## Tough talking

No matter how tough the questions you are asked, if you're well prepared you should be able to take them in your stride. Once you've absorbed the groundrules throughout this chapter (and the last two), you should be able to answer any question – even one you hadn't specifically prepared for. Just remember:

- Stay calm.
- Take your time to answer tricky questions.
- Don't argue.
- Don't admit to any significant weaknesses.
- Don't be drawn into criticizing anyone.

# 9 Your own questions

When the interviewer has asked you everything they want to, they'll invite you to ask them any questions you have. They are well aware that the interview is a two-way process, and they want to make sure that if they decide to offer you the job, you'll want to take it. So they want a chance to reassure you on any points which may be bothering you.

If you are tempted at this point to feel that the interview is all but over and you can relax, think again. The questions you do and don't ask can say a great deal about you, and can still influence the interviewer's decision on whether to offer you the job. And not asking any questions won't let you off the hook – having no questions at all will make you appear unenthusiastic and lacklustre. In any case, you really should have questions. There are things your interviewer won't have told you which you should want to find out about if you're serious about this job.

## Did you know?

Professional interviewers really are impressed by enthusiasm – it can tip the balance in your favour if there's a close decision between you and one other impressive candidate. So when asked if you have any questions, start by saying, 'Yes, I have. I'd certainly be interested in joining this company, and there are a couple of things I'd like to know ...'

So what sort of questions will give a good impression, and which ones will put interviewers off? Let's start by looking at the type of questions you should avoid; you should be able to see the linking factor between all of them. Here are some typical examples:

- What will my salary be?
- What holiday entitlement will I get?
- How long do most people take for lunch?
- Would I get my own office?
- I need to drop the kids off at school on my way to work; would it be OK to start at 9.30?

As you can see, all these questions are focused on what you can get out of the organization, not what you can offer it. Now, I'm not suggesting that you don't want – and in some cases genuinely need – to find these things out. But none of them will matter unless you get the job. So worry about winning a job offer first; plenty of time then to discuss details like this – even practical matters of fitting your work around your home life.

## The questions

So there's a good list of the kind of things you shouldn't ask. And you shouldn't duck out of asking any questions at all, either. So if you've got to ask something, what should it be? Well, you need to ask questions which show you are enthusiastic about the organization and the job, and about what you can contribute. And you want to look intelligent, ambitious and committed.

You won't get time to ask dozens of questions, but you should reckon to ask at least two or three, and up to about half a dozen if they're reasonably brief and the interviewer doesn't show any signs of wanting to wind up the interview quickly. So look through the ideas that follow, and prepare a few relevant questions for your interview.

## Why has this vacancy come up?

This is a sensible question, and one which may have been covered earlier in the interview. But if it hasn't, you can ask it now. If there happens to be anything fishy going on, you will probably pick up clues from the answer. Most vacancies are entirely reasonable, but some people leave because the job is frustrating or a certain colleague or superior is impossible to work with. If this is the case, you want to know. If you receive a non-committal answer to your question – such as 'The person doing the job at the moment is leaving' – you might want to probe a little deeper.

There are two ways of doing this. One is to ask directly, 'Are they leaving for any reason that I need to know about?' If there is something you should know, it's going to be difficult for the interviewer to avoid telling you. If they do sidestep the question again, that in itself should be a clue to you that things aren't right. If your interviewer is getting defensive and you don't want to appear pushy, you can always let the matter drop for now. If you are offered the job, however, pursue it further at that stage.

The other, less forward approach to gleaning more about why the present incumbent is leaving is simply to ask how long they have been in the job. If they've only been there a few months, it's reasonable to ask why they are moving on so soon. If they have been there for several years, the chances are they were simply ready for a change. However, if you detect any defensiveness in your interviewer you should still make a note to follow up this question if you're offered the job.

## Do you promote internally when possible?

If you're asking questions about promotion, that shows you're keen to do well and you plan to move up the organization. As a supplementary question, you can also ask whether the company or the division is expanding at the moment.

## What opportunities are there to gain extra qualifications or experience?

You want to be careful with questions about training if you've applied for the job setting yourself up as an expert in your field. But if this isn't the case, or if you are a professional such as an accountant or legal specialist who would expect to add to your qualifications, go ahead and ask. Again, it shows you want to improve your career prospects and increase your value to the company.

### Selection savvy

Bear in mind, when you start asking questions, that most interviewers will resent it if they feel you are trying to take control and start, in effect, to interview *them*. So remain deferential and make sure you don't inadvertently take over. It helps, for example, to start questions with phrases like, 'May I ask …?' rather than launching into an interrogative , 'Tell me …' style of approach.

## What will be the top priority in this job over the next six months?

This is an extremely useful question to know the answer to, and it also shows that your focus is on the overall objectives of the job, so you're less likely to get bogged down in day-to-day routine and fail to meet your targets. It also has the psychological advantage of projecting into the future and inviting your interviewer to envisage you in the job.

If you have a second interview with someone else, it's well worth asking this question again. It's useful to see if there is a consistent view as to what your key objective should be.

## If I were offered this job, where would you see me in five years' time?

Again, you're asking your interviewer to imagine you in the job. You're also showing a long-term commitment to the company, and indicating that you'd want to progress upwards. The answer is also going to be very informative – how fast do careers move in this organization, and in what direction? You need this information if you're offered the job.

## Where does the company want to be in five years' time?

Interviewers are particularly impressed by questions about their organization, showing you have a wider interest than simply the narrow focus of your own job. So this is a great question to impress the interviewer with, as well as being something you really ought to want to know the answer to.

### Nobody expects the Spanish Inquisition ...

If some of these questions sound a little pushy to you, remember that the phrasing makes a big difference. It is certainly possible to ask, 'Do you have any reservations about my ability to do this job?' in a way which is firm – even a little aggressive. If you're a confident kind of person with a no-nonsense interviewer, this probably won't bother you. But if you feel uncomfortable asking such upfront questions, it is equally possible to ask it in a gentle, non-confrontational way.

Try asking the following questions out loud, changing the words if that helps. Find turns of phrase and variations of tone that enable you to feel comfortable with the question:

- Why has this vacancy come up?
- If I were offered this job, where would you see me in five years' time?
- Do you have any reservations about my ability to do this job?

You'll need to find your own style, but phrases such as 'May I ask ...?' and 'I was wondering ...' can help to soften a question without changing its meaning. Just make sure you don't sound apologetic or under-confident, so avoid phrases such as 'I hope you don't mind my asking ...'.

## Do you have any reservations about my ability to do this job?

This question can be prefixed with a confident statement along the lines of, 'I'm very interested in this job, and I believe I could do it well'. It may seem like a pushy question, but in fact, it's perfectly reasonable. You're a salesperson, selling yourself as the ideal employee in this post, and you need to know whether your buyer has any outstanding sales objections. Why shouldn't you ask?

If they say they have none, they are saying they have no reason not to offer you the job – a very useful admission to draw from them. If they *do* have reservations they'll have to express them, and you'll get a final chance to reassure them.

## When can I expect to hear from you?

This may have been covered already, but if not you should ask it. And make it your last question. Apart from the fact that you need to know this, it gives you another potential advantage. If they fail to get in touch by the date they say they will, it gives you a legitimate reason to contact them and chase them up.

Not only does this stop you being on tenterhooks for so long, it can have a practical use, too. What if you're offered another job in the interim? And suppose you have to give them a prompt answer? If you've been promised a response from this interview by a certain date it makes it easier to put gentle pressure on the interviewer to meet that deadline.

---

### Question time

Try to come up with questions you genuinely want to know the answers to – the ones in this chapter are not definitive, they are merely guides and suggestions. Save the practical questions about hours of work and all that stuff until you're offered the job (the interviewer may well tell you this anyway, without asking). Recognize that asking questions has a dual purpose:

- to acquire any additional information you need
- to impress your interviewer with your incisive, intelligent and focused approach.

Prepare your questions in advance and then practise them out loud – with a friend or colleague role playing the part of the interviewer if possible – until you find a way of asking them that you feel relaxed with.

---

# 10 Competency-based interviews

You may well be told to expect an assessment using competency-based interviewing. Or you may find the interviewer employing this style of interview without describing it to you as such; it may be incorporated into the standard interview.

So what does it mean? Well, it's an interview technique for assessing 'competencies' or behavioural skills which are central to the job you're applying for. In other words, it examines your abilities rather than your technical skills. The interviewer will use this method to judge, in depth, competencies such as:

- teamwork
- planning ability
- coping with change
- self motivation
- presentation skills
- customer service
- problem solving.

## What competencies will they assess?

There's no need to panic that your interviewer will subject you to stringent cross-examination on a topic you're totally unprepared for. You can easily prepare because you should know what they're going to ask you about. How? Because they will use competency-based interview techniques to assess the competencies or skills which are central to the job; and they will have told you what these are in the recruitment ad, the application form and any information pack they sent you with the application form.

Job ads are full of phrases such as 'the successful candidate will demonstrate good interpersonal skills / calmness under pressure / the ability to multi-task / determination / excellent influencing skills…' There are your clues; and pretty big clues they are too. These are the 'competencies' you'll be asked about in depth at the interview.

## What sort of questions will they ask?

Competency-based interviewing isn't a new, scary technique which will throw you off your stride (not if you're prepared, anyway). It's a technique that many interviewers have used in some way for years. Only now it's got a fancy name, and it has become more formalized and standardized.

The underlying premise behind competency-based interviewing is that the best indicator of how you will perform in future is how you have performed in the past. So the questions you'll be asked will all be designed to learn how you've handled previous situations which called for the same competencies.

Some interviews can be entirely competency-based, while other interviewers use this as just one part of the overall interview. The questions are generally well structured in advance, which means that everyone else is being asked exactly the same questions as you. Competency-based interviewing is regarded as being extremely fair for this reason: all the candidates are being assessed in the same way, against the same competencies, using the same questions. Your job is to make sure that your answers are more impressive than everyone else's.

Let's take one example – teamwork – and look at the kind of questions you can expect to answer. To establish whether you're a good team player your interviewer will ask you several questions around this competency, such as:

■ Describe a time when you had to work as part of a team to achieve a specific result.

- Have you ever witnessed conflict in a team you were part of? Tell me about it, and how you handled it?
- Have you ever been irritated or frustrated by someone in your team? What did you do about it?
- What role do you tend to take in a team?
- Have you ever worked in a poorly motivated team? Tell me what you did to improve the team's morale.

As you can see, the answers to these questions can tell the interviewer a great deal about your past behaviour as a member of a team which, in turn, will indicate how you're likely to behave as a team member if they offer you this job. Such in-depth questioning around each competency gives them a very solid impression of your abilities.

The interviewer may probe you for more information about these questions, and you may be asked to discuss your answers.

Here's another example, this time questions you might expect to be asked about your customer service skills:

- What do you least like about dealing with customers?
- Has a customer ever criticized you personally? How did you deal with it?
- Tell me about a time when you exceeded your customer's expectations.
- Describe the angriest customer complaint you've ever received. How did you deal with it?

## Do your research

Go through all the literature you've received about the job you're applying for, and note down every competency that is mentioned as being a requisite for the job. Look at:

- the recruitment ad
- the application form

- the job description

- any other information the employer has sent you.

Sometimes the information will be spelt out, for example 'the success-ful candidate will be able to...'. However you may have to extrapolate information from the job description. This shouldn't be difficult as it will be clear whether this job particularly requires teamwork, organizational skills, the ability to learn fast, project management skills and so on.

## How should you answer the questions?

To begin with, you need to prepare your answers before you ever reach the interview. You've already identified the competencies you're likely to be asked about. For each one of these you need to:

- Work out the kind of questions you're likely to be asked (along the lines of the examples above).

- Come up with *more than one* example from your past experience to illustrate each competency. This will show the interviewer that you have broad experience of this kind of thing. One example that you constantly come back to for every question on that competency will give the impression that you don't have a lot of experience. If each set of questions gives rise to examples from a couple of different jobs or more, and maybe a non-work example too, the interviewer will be left with the idea that you're an old hand at demonstrating this competency.

- Prepare real anecdotes of your past experience to illustrate any question about each competency that is likely to arise. To take the example above of customer service, you need to think through what was your most difficult customer, when you've been person-ally criticized, when you've been let down by your suppliers and had to take the rap, when a complaint has been fully justified and so on, ready for whatever question you may be asked. What you *don't* want is for the interviewer to say, 'Tell me about a time when…' and for you to have to reply, 'Umm, well, let me think. I'm sure it's happened to me…'.

## Selection savvy

Remember that you can use examples from outside work. They can be just as good an indicator of how you behave and what skills you have. If you've been more nervous before going on stage at the local theatre than before any presentation you've given, or you have a very tricky bunch of people to deal with on your local conservation trust committee, bring these examples into the interview.

Once you've gone through the process of identifying the likely questions and preparing examples and anecdotes to illustrate how you handled them, you need to practise giving these answers out loud. You can do this in private or with a friend role playing the interviewer. The important thing is that you don't only identify the examples you plan to use, but you also think through how to put those examples into words.

# The interview

OK, you're ready for the interview. You've done all your preparation, you know what to say and how to say it, in order to demonstrate that you are ideally skilled in all the key competencies and the best person for the job on any objective competency-based measure.

All you need to do once you arrive at the interview is to select the most relevant example you can to answer each question. Bear in mind that the interviewer wants to know what you personally did in the situation you're describing, not what the team as a whole did, or what you think you could have done. They want to know about you, and about what actually happened.

The interviewer will want fairly full (but not rambling) answers to the questions, and will want you to be as specific as possible. They don't want a broad, 'We used to have some tricky customers…', they'll want to hear, 'There was one time when a particular customer turned up at the front desk, really angry...'. You can expect them to ask you more questions around each answer and to probe in detail. This doesn't mean that they're unhappy with your first answer; it's normal for this kind of interview.

If you've done your preparation well you should do extremely well at this kind of interview. It's all about being ready with specific and relevant examples to demonstrate your skill in the areas which are important to this job.

---

### Don't catch yourself carping

Many of the questions you're asked in a competency-based interview will be about tricky situations. After all, these are the ones which really test your ability. And many of these will be tricky because of the people involved. If you're asked to describe a time when you've had to cope with a difficult customer, colleague or boss, it's easy to find yourself criticizing the person concerned: 'I used to have this bastard of a boss,' or 'We had this grumpy, irritating customer who used to drive us all mad.'

However, bitching and criticizing doesn't put you in a good light, as we've seen already, and you need to avoid doing it in the answers you give to interview questions. The way to do this is to avoid making any value judgements. If your boss was short tempered that day, you can say so. But don't say he was a bad tempered difficult boss. You have the advantage that you're talking about individual specific situations, so you don't have to comment on people's long term behaviour. You can simply say, 'My boss had rather a short fuse that day,' or 'The customer was very angry,' and leave it at that.

If you want to go one further you can also, where it's appropriate, briefly excuse the other person's behaviour to emphasize subtly that you're not being bitchy. For example, 'My boss was very short staffed that day and understandably had rather a short fuse,' or 'The customer was justifiably angry.'

# 11 Psychometric tests

If you've never faced a psychometric test before, they can be a bit scary. In fact, if you *have* faced them before, they can still be scary. But they needn't be, once you understand how they work and what they're for. If you're the best person for the job, a psychometric test will reinforce rather than undermine your position.

## Did you know?

An increasing number of organizations are using psychometric testing to back up other selection procedures (such as interviews). They are most popular as part of the selection process for graduates and for managers at all levels, where you are more likely than not to be asked to complete a personality questionnaire.

So what exactly is a psychometric test? They fall broadly into four categories:

- *Ability tests,* which test your general ability at broad skills such as numeracy. IQ tests fall into this category.
- *Aptitude tests,* which relate to job-specific skills such as selling or managing.
- *Personality tests,* which assess your personality type.
- *Motivation questionnaires,* which assess what drives you and what your relevant attitudes are.

Although these are termed 'tests' they do not have pass and fail marks. They are simply intended to give an indication of your ability or personality and – especially in the case of personality testing – there are no right or wrong answers. Professional interviewers do not use psychometric tests in isolation, but only as a backup to other selection methods.

# Preparing for tests

It's pretty rare to be asked to sit a psychometric test of any kind without warning. Almost invariably you will be told when you are invited for interview that you will be asked to take a test, often later the same day. Or you may be told at the end of the interview that the interviewer would like you to sit a test (or possibly a battery of tests).

The interviewer should also explain fully what they intend to use the test for, and how it fits in with the rest of the recruitment process. On top of that, they should also make sure that you understand the test itself – what you're supposed to do, how long the test will last, that sort of thing.

## Selection savvy

If you have any medical condition that might inhibit your ability to do the test (such as dyslexia, or partial blindness, for example), then do explain this to the interviewer. They should be able to work around this quite easily, so long as they know.

Managers unused to interviewing are less likely to use tests, but of course you could find yourself with one of these interviewers and a test that they haven't explained properly. So feel free to ask questions, as soon as you know you will be asked to take a psychometric test. Even experienced interviewers may not tell you everything you want to know. So here's the sort of thing that is regarded as quite acceptable to ask:

- What kind of tests will you be taking – ability, aptitude, personality, motivation?

- How will you be asked to take the test – verbally, written, on the internet?

- How will the test fit in with the recruitment process as a whole?

- What tests will you be taking? There are plenty of tests out there, all with names, and they should be happy to tell you which ones they are using.

- Are there any test guides you can look at? Test guides give examples of what to expect. If there aren't any, ask the interviewer for samples. It's just like doing mock exams before you take your GCSE or A levels – looking at comparable examples is considered prudent preparation, not cheating.

- What feedback can you expect after the test? At the end of the test, and once the results have been assessed, you should be given some kind of feedback by the interviewer or a colleague of theirs trained in such things.

Once you have this information, you start to feel happier about the tests. You can use the internet, if you're connected, to find out more about the test you've been told you'll be taking. Either log on to the test producer's website or, if you don't know their web address, simply key the name of the test into a search engine. Many test producers give sample tests on their websites for you to practise (some charge for this service, others don't).

### Just imagine...

... running out of time. If you haven't sat a timed test in a while, and you're a little rusty, practise doing any kind of written exercise within a specified time limit. Otherwise you might be doing brilliantly at the test, and you're about half-way through, when you're told that your time is up.

### Whoops...

When it comes to the test itself, make sure you're ready for it, and don't forget your glasses or anything else you might need. The assessment experts ASE recommend the following top ten points when taking a psychometric test of any kind:

1 Try to keep calm and read instructions carefully.

2 Don't skim read any instructions. It's important to be clear about how to answer the questions.

3 Always complete the practice questions at the start of any assessment – ask your test administrator if there is anything you don't understand before you start the test.

4 Plan your time to answer as many questions as possible.

5 Don't spend too long on a single question – you can always go back at the end.

6 Check that the question number being completed matches the one on the answer sheet.

7 When assessing difficult multiple-choice questions start by ruling out those that are most unlikely to be correct.

8 If you change an answer make sure that it is clear.

9 If in doubt give your best estimate.

10 If you finish early go back and review your answers.

Reproduced with kind permission of ASE, Cheswick Centre, 414 Chiswick High Road, London, W4 5TF, a division of The NFER-NELSON Publishing Company Limited, Darville House, 2 Oxford Road East, Windsor, Berkshire SL4 1DF, England, publishers of a wide selection of psychometric assessments.

## Just imagine...

... what can happen if you don't follow the instructions carefully. Most tests are perfectly straight, but a few can have hidden catches. In one notorious test, candidates are asked to read the whole paper before answering any of the questions. Obviously almost no one takes any notice of this. But as you finish the paper, you find that the fine print at the end tells you not to write down any of your answers.

**Whoops...**

# Ability and aptitude tests

These tests measure specific skills and give a score which tells your potential employer what your level of ability is, or what your potential for learning new skills is. Research has shown that ability and aptitude tests are an excellent guide to future performance, so it's no surprise employers use them with increasing frequency.

These tests are not general knowledge tests, they are aimed at assessing your ability to reason or think logically. A few tests are broad in scope, but many focus on specific skills such as verbal skills, numeracy, data interpretation and so on, with verbal and numerical tests the most popular.

You'll find that ability and aptitude tests feel a bit like exams. You may have half an hour to answer the questions, which are often multiple choice. They frequently get more difficult as you go through the test, and there may well be more questions than you can answer. If this happens, don't panic. The proportion of answers you get right is more important than the number of questions you complete.

## Did you know?

Scores for aptitude and ability tests are rated against other people's past performance. So if everyone finds the test hard, you will be assessed in relation to everyone else, not simply given a low score. Equally, if very few people have time to complete all the questions, this will be taken into account in your score.

So how important are ability and aptitude tests in relation to the rest of the selection process? You can gauge this by when in the selection process you take the test. The earlier you take it, the more important it generally is. If it is the very first thing you are asked to do – even before attending an interview – it is probably a screening process; you will only be invited for interview if you reach a certain score. The later in the process the test comes, the more it will be treated as one of only many parts of the recruitment process.

## Preparing for aptitude and ability tests

We've already seen that it's useful to practise for these tests by getting hold of sample questions or practice papers. But what else can you do? Here are a couple of tips:

- Practise not only with test papers but also with other related exercises such as brain teasers and puzzles.

- For aptitude tests in particular, play word games and do mathematical puzzles.

- Practise your mental arithmetic, and things like long division and multiplication.

- For a numeracy test, find out if you'll be allowed to take a calculator into the test. If so, remind yourself (if necessary) of how to use a calculator to work out such things as percentages.

If you've been asked to take any aptitude or ability tests, you'll want to practise as we've already established. Here are a few sample questions to give you an idea of the sort of thing you might encounter. They are set by one of the leading producers of such tests, SHL Group, who have more examples on their website (*www.shlgroup.com*), along with online practice tests (for which they make a charge). Answers to each are given at the end of the chapter.

*Verbal example question*

In this test you are required to evaluate each statement in the light of the passage. Read through the passage and evaluate the statements according to the rules:

| | | |
|---|---|---|
| **True** | If the statement follows logically from the information or opinions contained in the passage | **Answer A** |
| **False** | If the statement is obviously false from the information or opinions contained in the passage | **Answer B** |
| **Cannot say** | If you cannot say whether the statement is true or false without further information | **Answer C** |

*Most banks and building societies adopt a 'no smoking' policy in customer areas in their branches. Plaques and stickers are displayed in these areas to draw attention to this policy. The notices are worded in a 'customer friendly' manner, though a few customers may feel their personal freedom of choice is being infringed. If a customer does ignore a notice, staff are tolerant and avoid making a great issue of the situation. In fact, the majority of customers now expect a 'no smoking' policy in premises of this kind. After all, such a policy improves the pleasantness of the customer facilities and also lessens fire risk.*

| | | | |
|---|---|---|---|
| 'No smoking' policies have mainly been introduced in response to customer demand | A | B | C |
| All banks and building societies now have a 'no smoking' policy | A | B | C |
| There is no conflict between a 'no smoking' policy and personal freedom of choice for all | A | B | C |
| A 'no smoking' policy is in line with most customers' expectations in banks and building societies | A | B | C |

© SHL Group plc. This text has been reproduced here with the permission of SHL Group plc.

*Numerical example question*

The numerical question which follows is multiple choice; you are given several possible answers. When you have selected your answer, circle the appropriate letter.

*Newspaper readership*

| DAILY NEWSPAPERS | Readership (millions) | | Percentage of adults reading each paper in 1990 | |
|---|---|---|---|---|
| | 1981 | 1990 | Male | Female |
| The Daily Chronicle | 3.6 | 2.9 | 7 | 6 |
| Daily News | 13.8 | 9.3 | 24 | 18 |
| The Tribune | 1.1 | 1.4 | 4 | 3 |
| The Herald | 8.5 | 12.7 | 30 | 23 |
| Daily Echo | 4.8 | 4.9 | 10 | 12 |

**1** Which newspaper was read by a higher percentage of females than males in 1990?

| A | B | C | D | E |
|---|---|---|---|---|
| *The Tribune* | *The Herald* | *Daily News* | *Daily Echo* | *The Daily Chronicle* |

**2** What was the combined readership of the *Daily Chronicle, Echo* and *Tribune* in 1981?

| A | B | C | D | E |
|---|---|---|---|---|
| 10.6 | 8.4 | 9.5 | 12.2 | 7.8 |

**3** Which newspaper showed the largest change in female readership between 1981 and 1990?

| A | B | C | D | E |
|---|---|---|---|---|
| *Daily Echo* | *The Tribune* | *The Herald* | *The Daily Chronicle* | Cannot say |

©SHL Group plc. This text has been reproduced here with the permission of SHL Group plc.

*Diagrammatical example question*

The diagrammatic questions which follow are multiple choice. For each question, you are given several possible answers. Each problem in this test consists of a series of diagrams, on the left of the page, which follow a logical sequence. You are to choose the next diagram in the series from the five options on the right. Then indicate your answer by circling it.

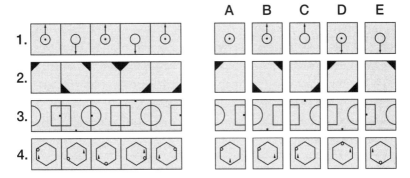

© SHL Group plc. This text has been reproduced here with the permission of SHL Group plc.

# Personality tests and motivation questionnaires

These tests are very different from ability and aptitude tests because there are no right or wrong answers (you may be pleased to know) and the tests are not generally timed. They simply aim to assess what kind of person you are. The point of this is to see how suited you are to the type of work you'd be doing, how you would fit in with the company culture, and how well you would mesh with the team you'd be part of.

Since you have absolutely no idea what the organization is looking for in terms of personality type, there's no point in giving anything but truthful answers to these questions. In any case, these tests benefit you as well. If you really don't suit the corporate culture or the type of work you'd be doing, you probably wouldn't want the job. The kind of thing these tests will identify include:

- what motivates you
- your attitude to life and work
- how you relate to other people
- how you handle emotions
- how you approach problems.

Motivation questionnaires are similar to personality tests but they focus more specifically on what drives you, how long you maintain your energy levels for a particular task, what situations tend to motivate you more or less, and so on. They are more often used for staff development (once you're in the job) than for recruitment, but you may encounter them during a selection process.

Here's a brief example of the kind of questions you might find in a personality questionnaire:

*Rating statements*

In this example you are asked to rate yourself on a number of phrases or statements. After reading each statement you should mark yourself according to the following rules:

Select Circle 1    If you strongly disagree with the statement

Select Circle 2    If you disagree with the statement

Select Circle 3    If you are unsure

Select Circle 4    If you agree with the statement

Select Circle 5    If you strongly agree with the statement

|  | **Strongly disagree** | **Disagree** | **Unsure** | **Agree** | **Strongly agree** |
|---|---|---|---|---|---|
| I enjoy meeting new people | (1) | (2) | (3) | (4) | (5) |
| I like helping people | (1) | (2) | (3) | (4) | (5) |
| I sometimes make mistakes | (1) | (2) | (3) | (4) | (5) |

## Testing, testing

Psychometric tests are pretty straightforward once you know what to expect. You should be given warning if you're going to be asked to do a test, and you should also be given plenty of explanations, practice questions, and so on.

You can make sure you get plenty of practice by finding out more about the test you'll be sitting (ask for their names) from the test producer's website. There are also several books available which give you details of most of the popular tests on the market.

When it comes to taking the tests:

- Stay calm.

- Read the questions and instructions carefully.

- Plan your time to answer as many questions as possible.

Answers to test questions
Verbal: C, B, A
Numerical: D, C, E
Diagrammatic: E, B, D, D

# 12 Assessment centres

Assessment centres are another of the tools employers sometimes use – alongside interviews and psychometric tests – to assess candidates. They are really another form of test, but this time on a more practical level. You undertake some kind of exercise – or perhaps several – such as group discussion exercises, role plays or team project exercises. (If you are also taking psychometric tests, these may take place at the assessment centre.) An assessor, or a team of assessors, will observe you during the exercise.

## Did you know?

The term assessment centre is misleading, since it isn't a physical location at all, but a process. It may well take place at the employer's premises, although it can take place at an external location.

Like ability and aptitude testing, assessment centres are one of the most accurate predictors of future performance. They are also, you'll be pleased to know, reckoned to be an extremely fair and objective method of assessing candidates. So again, if you really are the best person for the job, you can be confident it will show.

There are several different types of exercise you might be asked to perform. The key thing to remember is that even when the exercise is geared towards an end result, such as making a decision, the way you carry out the exercise will generally be at least as important as your final result. This means that you should make sure:

■ The assessors can see what preparation you have done by making notes where appropriate.

■ You indicate how you have arrived at any conclusions.

There are countless assessment centre exercises you might be asked to do, but here is a quick guide to the main types you might encounter.

■ *In tray.* This is just what it sounds like. You're given the hypothetical in tray of the person whose job you would be taking over. You have to go through everything in it, and mark on each piece of correspondence how you would handle it and what action you would take arising from it. Since these annotations are all the assessors have to go on, you need to make sure you mark down anything which might be useful or relevant.

■ *Case study.* Here, you are given plenty of factual information about a business issue on which you have to make a decision. The information may be unclear in places. You have to assess the information and arrive at a decision, which you then relay to the assessors either in a brief written report or as a short presentation. Although it is important to make a decision if you are briefed to do so, your approach to the issue is as important as your conclusion.

■ *Group discussion.* This is very similar to the case study except that you have to make a decision or recommendation – or perhaps several – in a group together with other candidates. Sometimes you are each given a particular role to play, but you may all be given the same information.

■ *Interview role play.* In this exercise you are given a brief on a meeting you are about to have with a role player. You should use the brief to plan the meeting – the way you do this will be a significant part of the overall assessment. (You'll be given anything up to 30 minutes to prepare.) The meeting, as your brief will tell you, will involve either discussing an issue with the role player, or using them to help you collect information about the issue. Either way, you will be expected to use the information, or the results of the discussion, to reach a decision on the issue.

**Selection savvy**

All tests and exercises are, essentially, just another way of finding out about you, the same as the interview itself. The aim is not to torture you, trick you or put you through the hoop, but simply to establish whether you are the best candidate for the job. So your best approach is to take them in your stride, be yourself and carry out the exercises as honestly and as well as you can.

# Team tests

If the employer is particularly keen to know how you fit into a team, they may ask you to take part in some kind of team test. This kind of test generally lasts all day or even over a couple of days. It might involve anything from hiking across the moors to building a model of the Eiffel Tower out of paperclips. You will be observed and assessed throughout the test.

One positive point to bear in mind here is that these tests are expensive to run, and your prospective employer wouldn't be spending their money unless they felt the job warranted it and you were worth the investment. So simply being asked to take part in the test is a confidence boost.

Unless you're applying for a job as a park ranger, it's unlikely your prospective employer gives two hoots whether you can hike across the moors. It is also unlikely that they really need a model of the Eiffel Tower in paperclips. No, what they want to know is how you function in a team. You can't spend the time trying to be someone you're not – and if you got the job on that basis you wouldn't be happy in it anyway. You are likely to be put under sufficient pressure that you'll have a hard time putting on a complete act for the duration in any case.

So be aware that it's your team performance that counts, not the project you've been set. Be yourself but avoid the extremes which may deter the assessors from recommending you:

- Don't take over officiously and become too bossy (although if the team genuinely defers to you as its leader that's fine).

- Don't be so quiet and reserved that you seem uninvolved. Make sure you make enough of a contribution to be assessed on.

- Don't argue with other team members. If conflict arises, play the diplomat and be seen to be trying to improve matters.

- Don't opt out and refuse to play the game, saying 'This is stupid! What's the point of building an Eiffel Tower anyway?'

- If there are other teams competing with yours, it's a good thing to show a competitive streak, but not to the point of ruthlessness. Adopt the approach that, 'It's only a game, but all things being equal we'd prefer to win it and we'll give it our best shot.' You are not more likely to get the job because your team was first to complete its paperclip construction. It's how you play the game that counts.

Apart from being the diplomat, the most useful roles you can take on in the team, to impress your assessors, are:

- Keep the team focused on the objective: 'Hey, guys, does it really matter how we string the paperclips together? Let's concentrate on getting the tower built – we can each string them together in our own way.'

- Summarize how the team is doing from time to time: 'So we've worked out how to construct the thing, and we've decided not to try and incorporate a working elevator. That means we need to think about allocating tasks next.'

## Good exercise

Assessment centres are a good method of judging your ability to do the job fairly and objectively. The way you approach the exercises can be as important as any final conclusion you reach, or decision you make. Some exercises are solo ones, while others you will do with a role player, or in a group with other candidates.

If you are asked to take part in a team test you are probably being assessed on your ability to work in a team, especially if the exercise itself isn't relevant to the job you're applying for. So it matters relatively little how well the team completes the exercise, but a great deal how you interact with the other members of your team. So follow the basic guidelines:

- Don't either take over or remain uninvolved.

- Don't start arguments; help to resolve them.

- Keep the team focused on its objective.

- Summarize the team's progress when it seems useful to do so.

# 13 Second interviews

Interviewers don't hold second interviews because they can't decide who to offer the job to and they want another look at the candidates. The second interview is an opportunity to find out more about the candidates, or to enable someone more senior to interview a shortlist of candidates. Or maybe you were recruited through an agency who interviewed you initially, so this is the first time you've met the employer. Whichever is the case, it's not going to be a straight repeat of the first interview.

## Selection savvy

Don't forget the basics when you go for your second interview. As well as following all the guidelines for first interviews, you should also:

- Wear a different outfit from last time – it looks as if a smart appearance is second nature to you, rather than that you have only one smart outfit which you drag out of the back of the wardrobe for interviews.

- Remember, and use, the names of all the people you met last time. Make sure you recognize them all and greet them, 'Nice to see you again'.

- Remember to take the right paperwork and your portfolio samples with you.

You may find you are asked to undergo psychometric tests, assessment centre exercises or a technical interview alongside your second interview; all quite formal. On the other hand, an interview with a senior colleague or manager of your original interviewer can be quite informal, as they simply want to ascertain that the first interviewer made an accurate assessment of you.

If there is an outstanding concern from your first interview, it is likely to be aired at a second interview. Your interviewers may be worried if you have significantly less experience than the other candidates, or are very different from them in some other way. Or maybe they are concerned that you are overqualified. Interviewers often put one 'wildcard' candidate on the shortlist, and it could be you. So they need reassurance that you are the right person for the job and that any worrying features of your application are in fact strengths.

It's very possible that the interviewer at your second interview will put these concerns to you straight. But if they don't it should be quite obvious where they need reassuring. Remember, they called you back for a second interview so they obviously didn't consider that your lack of experience – or whatever bothers them – made you a write-off. And they must have thought you had considerable strengths elsewhere to shortlist you despite their misgivings. In other words, they *want* to be reassured that you can do the job.

You are likely to be asked a lot of questions directly related to your past performance at a second interview. So be ready for questions such as:

- What improvements have you introduced in your current job?
- What have you done to increase productivity?
- What has been your biggest success?
- And your biggest mistake?
- How have you increased the profitability of your department?

If you have management experience, you're also likely to be asked about this, including questions such as whether you have done your own training, recruitment, and so on. If the job is going to require you to relocate, they are also likely to ask how you feel about this, and how it will affect your family.

# Have a drink …

Many second interviews can be very informal affairs over lunch or dinner, or even over a few drinks at the wine bar. In this case, your interviewer (or there may be several) are largely looking to see how well you fit in and how easily you get on with people.

However relaxed the atmosphere becomes, never forget that you are on trial. Make sure you behave well and make easy conversation, but don't be tempted to give away anything about yourself that you wouldn't discuss at a formal interview. It isn't OK to let your hosts in on what a complete fluke that last big success of yours was in reality, or how funny you think it is to wind up junior staff by phoning and pretending to be the MD in a bad mood.

**Just imagine...**

… you've had a drink or two too many, and your hosts start talking about the biggest disasters of their careers. Then they ask about yours. They seem like friendly, amusing companions, so you tell them …

**Whoops...**

And most important of all, don't drink too much. Show you drink in moderation, but don't reach the point where it noticeably affects your behaviour (or your volume) in any way. If you are teetotal, obviously you won't want to drink. But don't give your interviewer the impression you are a reformed alcoholic; it won't go down well however long ago you gave up the booze.

## Second chance

A second interview is not a repeat of the first interview. It's a chance for your potential employers to find out more about you, or for someone new (and probably more senior than the last interviewer) to meet you. If there are any outstanding concerns about your candidature, they will be aired at this interview. You can also expect to be asked plenty of questions about your achievements in your most recent jobs.

If you are invited to lunch or dinner by your interviewer, be relaxed and friendly but never drop your guard. You are permanently on trial, even if it doesn't feel like it.

# part three

# after
# the
# interview

# 14 What to do while you're waiting to hear

You will probably feel a strong sense of relief once the interview is over. But just because the interview is over, it doesn't mean there's nothing more you can do. So as soon as you get back home from the interview, you'll need to do two things:

- Write a letter of thanks to the interviewer.
- Make notes.

## Saying thank you

I know this sounds depressingly like that endless round of 'thank-you' letters parents make small children write after Christmas and birthdays. But you need to write and thank the interviewer as soon as possible, since you want your letter to arrive before they make their decision. In order to make sure you're in time, you can always e-mail it, especially if you know they're going to make their decision quickly. Your thank-you letter has two purposes:

1 It enables you to remind the interviewer who you are, in much the same way an advertisement does.

2 It gives you a chance to mention (*briefly*) anything important you missed saying at the interview itself.

Since you will almost certainly be the only candidate who writes following the interview, it will do a lot to bring your name to the interviewer's attention, even if you had slipped down the list. It can make the difference, for example, between whether or not you get on to the shortlist for final interview. It shows you are keen on the job, committed and courteous with it.

So what's the letter going to say? It should say something along the lines of: 'Thank you for seeing me this morning. I very much enjoyed meeting you and I would like to confirm that I am still very interested in the post. I look forward to hearing from you.'

You may also want to add a brief note along the lines of: 'By the way, we discussed the possibility of working overseas, and I forgot to mention that I have previously taken evening language courses in both French and Spanish.' There's no need to add this kind of information unless there's something important you feel you omitted to say, and a single sentence will do fine. This is no place to launch into a long, defensive ramble because you think the interviewer had some reservation about your suitability and you feel like repeating what you've already said at the interview.

## Selection savvy

As with your application, your letter or e-mail needs to look as professional as possible. The standards for e-mail layout are fairly simple, but if you write a letter you'll need to make sure it looks smart and professional, or its positive effects will be seriously diluted.

# Making notes

Now, there's one more thing you'll need to do while you're waiting to hear: make notes about the interview. Any general points you note about how it went will help with other interviews – do you feel you were well prepared, were you confident enough, did you ramble too much, were you too flippant, did you answer questions fluently? These are useful points to note for yourself so you can handle your next interview even better.

There's another reason, too, for making notes. You may get a second interview. In case this happens you need to note:

- the names of your interviewer and anyone else you met
- any questions you feel you could have dealt with better (so you can prepare for next time)
- any reservations you suspect the interviewer may have been left with
- anything you wish you had said but didn't
- anything which seemed to impress them and will therefore be worth reinforcing next time.

---

### Hanging on

Make a good impression on your interviewer by writing a *brief* letter of thanks for seeing you. This will put you one up on most if not all the other candidates. And prepare for making a good impression next time too, by writing notes on how you feel you performed, and on anything you'll need to remember if you're called for a second interview.

# 15 What to do if you get the job

Congratulations – you've been offered the job. If you want it, accept it happily – subject to negotiations, which we'll look at in a moment. If you know you don't want it – you hated the company or you've got a better offer – that's fine too. Turn the job down, but do it politely. You never know when you might encounter people again, and it won't help if you once told them, however honestly, that they could stick their job and you wouldn't work for them if they paid you a million pounds.

## Selection savvy

Technically, your new job isn't guaranteed until you have been offered it in writing, with a contract stipulating pay and conditions, and you have returned a written acceptance. So don't hand in your notice until this process is complete, otherwise you could end up with no job at all.

## Bad timing

The problem comes, however, when you're offered a job while you're still waiting to find out if you're going to get a better offer from someone else. You don't want to say yes and then miss out on the better job. But you don't want to say no if you might *not* be offered the other job. Hmmm.

Your first response in this situation should be to play for time. Say you're delighted to be offered the job and please can you get back to them in, say, 24 hours. It's not going to be reasonable to leave it too long, and they'll guess what's going on if you ask for several days to decide. No one wants to be second best, so don't let them know you're hoping for a better offer. If they ask why you need time to decide, you can say that you want to talk it over with your family. Or simply say that taking on a new job is a big decision and you don't like to rush big decisions. They can't argue with that.

It's perfectly reasonable to get in touch with your preferred employer at this stage and explain the problem. They'll be pleased to be your first choice, and if they think everyone else wants to employ you too, that makes you look like an even better prospect. Don't expect an instant answer from them, but ask them if they could get back to you by tomorrow. They can always say no.

If this sounds like a good technique for getting an offer out of your first-choice employer even if you haven't really been offered another job, it isn't. Don't go there. If they were going to offer you the job anyway it may well persuade them to offer fast before they lose you. And it may work if they were tossing up between you and one other candidate. But if you were a borderline choice it is as likely to bounce them into saying no to you if they don't want the time pressure. But at least a firm no now leaves you free to accept the other offer, rather than wonder whether to turn it down and then risk ending up with nothing.

All sorts of circumstances, of course, can get in the way:

- It may be that your first-choice employer is nowhere near making a decision.

- Perhaps you haven't even been interviewed yet, or maybe they're still drawing up a shortlist for second interviews.

- Or maybe your first choice is internal promotion and you're reluctant to tell your boss that you've been applying for jobs elsewhere.

In any of these cases, I'm afraid there is nothing you can do but gamble. You'll have to weigh up how much you want this new job, how much you'd mind staying in the job you're in now, your chances of getting the job you *really* want, and so on. But remember – you're obviously employable and you can give a good interview (even when you've left it so late). The fact that this interviewer has offered you the job is a very good sign.

## Did you know?

The majority of employers check at least some of the candidate's qualifications before offering the job – it's reckoned that as many as 12 per cent of applicants make false or exaggerated claims about qualifications or work experience. Likewise, you can expect almost all employers to take up at least some references, and the majority will check all of them.

# Negotiating a deal

You should aim to leave any negotiations – on salary or other terms and benefits – until you have been offered the job. Once they've admitted that you are the candidate they want, it puts you in a much stronger negotiating position. So, as we've seen earlier, you should resist attempts to persuade you to talk about money until now.

You should expect to negotiate the contract rather than simply say yes to whatever they offer. It shows that you have a strong sense of your own value, and that you are no pushover. While this may mean they have to give more ground than they might want, in broader terms these are good qualities in an employee. In any case, they will expect to negotiate and they usually have some leeway to do so.

However, there's no point trying to get more than they can afford – you'll end up with stalemate and you'll lose the job at the last moment. Unless you don't want the job without a certain salary level, make sure you ask for what they can afford. So how much can they afford?

■ If a salary range has been quoted – or is quoted now – you can reasonably expect to get the top end of the range so long as you can demonstrate that you are worth it.

- If an approximate salary has been quoted you can assume that there is about a ten per cent leeway.

- If the job is one of those where there is a set pay scale which is inflexible, you can still negotiate over other benefits.

The more valuable you can demonstrate that you are, the better chance you will have of pushing the employer up to the higher end of their range. So if your qualifications or experience exceed what they said in their recruitment ads that they were looking for, that gives you a way to show that you're worth more than the average for the job. You need to prepare justifications for asking for the top end of the salary range, such as:

- 'I've not only gained my 706/1 qualification, as you specified in your recruitment material, but I also have my 706/2 and 706/3.'

- 'You were looking for two years' experience in computer programming, and in fact I've been programming computers since I was at school, and I've done it professionally for nearly four years now.'

- 'In addition to the experience and qualifications you asked for, I also speak French and Spanish fluently, which will be an important advantage since you have so many foreign clients.'

You've been offered this job because you can bring more to it than the other candidates, so presumably you have greater than average strengths. All you have to do is identify them, and use them as a negotiating tool.

## Selection savvy

Before you start your negotiations, you must know how much money you're looking for as a minimum. It might be the least you can afford to live on, or it might be the least you feel you are worth – any less and you'd rather not take the job. However you choose to define it, you must go into negotiations knowing your bottom line. If you don't, you're likely to be negotiated down below it.

You still haven't begun negotiating yet, but you're getting somewhere:

■ You've established your leverage for asking for a higher salary than their opening offer – that's all the ways in which you can demonstrate that you're worth more, from extra experience to useful additional skills.

■ You know what your bottom line is – the level below which you would turn down the job rather than accept the offer.

## Finding variables

There's one more thing you need to do before you start talking. You need to identify all the variables. In other words, all the other items you can negotiate over in addition to your salary. If you discuss money only, you're left haggling as if you were in a marketplace. You start a few thousand higher than they do and you each keep giving ground until you meet in the middle. But a salary negotiation can be far more sophisticated than that, and it's in your interests that it should be.

The variables are all the other factors you can bring into play to balance up with your salary. So if they offer you less than you wanted and seem unable or unwilling to budge, you can ask for extra holiday entitlement, or a home computer supplied by the employer. The more variables you have to play with, the more scope you both have for negotiating.

Have a look through this list of variables – there's room for you to add more at the end. In the middle column you can jot down what the offer is (if you know), and in the right-hand column you can write down what you want to negotiate for. Just remember, no one's going to give you everything. If you hold out for more commission, you'll have to concede something else such as a reduction in your basic salary. So fill this list in according to what you think is fair, reasonable and plausible, not according to some fantasy ideal.

| Variable | Current offer | Target |
|---|---|---|
| Salary | | |
| Bonus | | |
| Commission | | |
| Overtime | | |
| Profit sharing | | |
| Holiday entitlement | | |
| Personal leave days (dentist appointments, kids are home sick, etc.) | | |
| Medical/other insurance | | |
| Pension contribution | | |
| Stock options | | |
| Childcare contribution | | |
| Relocation costs | | |
| Company car | | |
| Company computer | | |
| Mobile phone | | |
| Travel allowance | | |
| Accommodation expenses | | |
| Health club membership | | |
| Start date for the job | | |
| Others: | | |

Once you've established what the variables are, you don't have to negotiate on everything. You may only negotiate on the ones you're really concerned about. But you know the others are there to bring into play if you start getting to a stalemate. If they simply won't move any further on salary or holidays, that may be time to ask for a computer or childcare allowance.

The thing is, employers can be very sensitive about paying you more than other comparable employees, in case word gets out. So they're much happier agreeing a salary no one's going to object to and making up the difference in other benefits. Equally, your salary is a straight cost, but it will cost them far less to provide you with a computer than it would cost you to buy one for yourself. You'll judge the value of the computer by the money it saves you buying your own, but the actual cost to them is far lower. So there are several reasons why you will often find it much easier to get them to concede benefits than salary.

## Negotiating techniques

The first rules of negotiating we've already covered:

- Establish your leverage.
- Know your bottom line.
- Find all the variables you can.

Once you're actually in conversation, there are three more rules you'll need to follow:

- Get all the cards on the table.
- Never give free concessions.
- Agree to all or nothing.

### Get all the cards on the table

If you're dealing with a tricky kind of negotiator, keen to negotiate the best deal they can for their company, there's one ace they'll be holding up their sleeve. You have to find out what it is. They may well have concessions they want from you before they will agree to a particular salary. They might want you to agree to start on a lower salary, or to take on extra responsibilities as well as those originally agreed. And if they are an underhand dealer, they will wait until the last minute to spring this on you. In other words, they will wait until you've pretty well agreed on the salary.

And then out of the blue: 'Oh, and I'd also like you to deal with your colleague Philippa's accounts while she's on maternity leave.' Now, it's not that you don't want the opportunity to show that you can take Philippa's accounts in your stride. It's just that if you do, that will increase your value even more, and with it the size of starting salary you deserve. But hang on, you'd almost finished negotiating, and your future employer knows that you were about to accept a salary somewhere in the middle of the advertised range. It's much harder now for you to backtrack and insist that you want a salary close to the top of their range. And they know it is.

## Selection savvy

The principle of good negotiating is that everyone should come out of it feeling like a winner. A negotiation alongside a job offer should be less confrontational than most – you're both on the same side after all – but if you're dealing with a naturally competitive negotiator they will still want to feel they've found the best person for the job, *and* at a knock-down price.

The way to prevent this is very simple: ask them to put all their cards on the table, and do the same thing yourself. That way, you can balance all the issues against each other. All you have to do is to say, for example: 'We need to talk about my salary, and I'd also like to discuss my holiday entitlement. Are there any other issues we need to discuss at the same time?' You've made it extremely difficult for them to keep back the fact that they want to talk to you about covering for Philippa while she's away. If they don't mention it, and then spring it on you later, you have the moral high ground and will find it much easier to insist that you go back over the other points you've agreed and revise them in the light of the new information.

**Selection savvy**

Don't forget that if you can't agree the starting salary you want, you may still be able to get the employer to agree to a salary review or even an agreed raise after a fixed period. It's not unreasonable for them to want to make sure you're as good as you seem. Get them to agree a specific salary raise at the review if you meet pre-agreed targets: 'How about £30,000 now, with an understanding that if I increase productivity by at least three per cent, that will go up to £32,000 at my six-month salary review?'

*Never give free concessions*

This is a simple but critical rule for negotiating. All it means is that if they ask you to lower the amount you're asking for, or concede that you will wait six months before getting a rise to the salary you want, you don't simply say yes; you trade the concession for a matching concession on their part:

■ If they say, 'I can offer you a salary review after only three months', you don't simply say, 'OK, then'. You say, 'So long as my salary increases by at least £1,000 if I successfully complete the probation period.'

■ 'When they say, 'I can only offer you a five per cent commission' you say, 'If we do it that way, the commission would need to be at least five per cent of gross.'

■ 'When they say, 'The holiday entitlement is only four weeks' you say, 'In that case I'd need at least five personal leave days a year.'

You've got the idea. This principle is crucial simply because it means that you end up with a better deal. Every time you lose something, you also gain something. Just make sure the concessions you gain roughly match the value of those you are giving.

**Selection savvy**

When you don't give free concessions, your future employer will soon learn that you are a tough negotiator. They'll think twice about asking concessions from you when they realize that every time they do, they have to give up something themselves. And in the long term, too, it's a good thing if they know you are no pushover when it comes to negotiating.

*Agree to all or nothing*

The way you reach a final settlement in your negotiation is by moving all the variables around until they balance. So, for example, if the salary is lower than you wanted, you will insist on a childcare allowance as well. Of course you could manage on a lower childcare allowance, but only if you get more personal leave days. And so on. It's as though all these factors are on sliding scales, and you are sliding one up as another goes down, keeping them all in a balance which produces a settlement you're happy with.

The one thing you mustn't do is to agree to any one variable before you agree to the rest of them. It would mean one of your sliders was stuck fast, and you couldn't adjust it to bring the whole thing into balance. This makes it far harder to agree on a final deal, and you may have to give more ground than you wanted on one of your other sliding scales to get a balance.

**Just imagine...**

... you've agreed your starting salary and your commission. And now your future employer tells you that the standard holiday entitlement in this company is a week less than you've been used to. Trouble is, you've got very little left to bargain with, having already agreed to most of the terms.

**Whoops...**

So you want to outlaw from the negotiation any comment such as: 'Right, we've agreed the basic salary. Now let's talk about the fringe benefits.' Don't agree any such thing, and if they try to railroad you with a comment like this just say, 'We haven't finalized the salary yet; I'm still considering it. But I'm happy to go on and discuss the other benefits.'

## The offer letter

Once the deal is finalized, you can expect an offer letter from your new employer. According to OneClickHR, this should outline clearly:

- the position that is being offered
- the remuneration
- the date of commencement of employment (if agreed)
- the location
- any conditions to which the offer is subject
- the timescale and procedure for acceptance/rejection of the offer.

Assuming all this tallies with what you've agreed, you're on your way. Respond to the offer in the way set out in the offer letter, which should be in writing to be legally binding, and good luck in your new job.

## Making the job right for you

When you're offered the job, you'll have to decide whether to take it. If you're not sure, for example if you're waiting to see if you get a better offer, you can ask for about 24 hours' decision time. But sooner or later you may simply have to take a gamble.

If you say yes to the job, you need to negotiate the best deal you can. Work within what you believe the employer can afford, and when you prepare to negotiate:

- Establish your leverage.

- Know your bottom line.

- Find all the variables you can.

Once negotiations are under way:

- Get all the cards on the table.

- Never give free concessions.

- Agree to all or nothing.

# 16 What if you miss out on the job?

However brilliant you are at interview, you won't always get the job. No one is right for every post, and inevitably there will be rejections. While you should be aware of any flaws in your performance, and make a note of them so you can work on them for next time, you shouldn't blame yourself if you don't get the job. If you've done all your preparation and followed all the advice in this book, you've done everything you could.

Well, that's fine if you've got lots of other promising interviews coming up, and maybe you had reservations anyway about the job you didn't get. But what if this was one of those jobs you were itching to get, and you feel strongly that you *were* the best person for it? Is it just tough luck, or is there anything you can do even after a rejection?

### Did you know?

Statistically, interviews are actually one of the least effective methods of selecting the best candidate (despite being the most popular). One of the main reasons for this is that they rely heavily on the skill and judgement of the interviewer, and not all interviewers are as skilled as they might be. According to Phil Boyle, Managing Director of Ramsey Hall Limited, a successful executive recruitment organization, 'If you find yourself being rejected for a job that you know you can do, put it down to a bad interviewer rather than any fault on your part.'

The good news is that it isn't unheard of for good candidates to land the job they're after even after they've been turned down for it. If you made it to the shortlist, or the final round of interviews, you were clearly thought capable of doing the job. It's just that your interviewer felt (rightly or wrongly) that one of the other candidates could do it even better.

## Just imagine...

... you didn't get the job, and you're very disappointed. Six weeks down the line, you're still looking for a change of job. Meanwhile, the candidate who got the job you were after finds they just don't fit in, and they decide to leave. The employer wonders who to offer the job to now. They've heard nothing from you since they turned you down, so they offer it instead to another shortlisted candidate who has been in touch with them.

### Whoops...

It's not uncommon for the successful candidate to last only a short time in the job. When this happens, the employers tend not to readvertise but to go back to one of the original candidates and offer them the job, if they're still available. Sometimes, another similar vacancy comes up within a couple of months and again, the employer is likely to approach any earlier candidates to see if they are still available.

If you were a good candidate, and you're still available, you'll be somewhere on their list of people to offer the job to next. But that's not good enough – you need to be at the top of the list. And you need them to know that you're still looking for the right job, and would be interested in anything they had to offer you.

So how are you going to get yourself to the top of that list? You need to write a letter of reply to your rejection letter, letting the interviewer know that you're still interested in any relevant vacancies they may have. You can be brief, saying something like: 'Thank you for letting me know the outcome of my application, and I'm sorry I was unsuccessful on this occasion. However, I was very impressed by your company and would still be interested in working for you. I'd be delighted if you would come back to me if things change, or if any other suitable posts arise in the near future.'

This kind of letter cannot help but impress your interviewer. Not only are you polite and enthusiastic about working for their organization, but you also know how to swallow your pride and continue to fight when the odds appear to be against you – which is a valuable talent to be able to demonstrate.

But even a letter like this won't work for ever. If a similar job comes up in six months' time, the employer will almost certainly go through the recruitment process again from scratch rather than give you a call. Unless... you've been in touch in the meantime.

So that's what you need to do, if you're still genuinely keen to work for that employer. And you may well be, especially if you're in a comfortable but, for example, not very challenging post. In this situation, you may well be applying for very few jobs, and perhaps even turning some down. You can afford to be choosy, and there are only a couple of organizations you really want to give up your present job for.

The best way to keep in touch is to contact the person who interviewed you every couple of months or so. You might phone, write or e-mail – or vary your method of contact each time. Whichever you do, be brief; don't irritate them or you'll do more harm than good. Simply tell them that you're still looking for the right job to come up, and you'd still be very interested in working for their organization. You're just letting them know that you're still out there – still keen.

**Smart exercise**

1  Go through your diary as soon as you're turned down for a job you really want, and make a note to contact your interviewer in a couple of months, if you haven't found a better job in the meantime.

2  Decide whether to phone or e-mail. If you decide to phone, plan what you will say in advance. If you e-mail, think as hard about how you word your communication as you would if it were a formal letter – it's very easy to treat e-mails so informally you don't properly think through what you're writing.

3  Each time you contact them, make a note to repeat the exercise in another two months.

That's all it takes to keep your name in the front of their mind, and to let them know you haven't taken another job yet. And if you're in any doubt that this could be worthwhile, just think of the number of ways it could still win you a job:

■ The candidate who took the job isn't happy in it and leaves.

■ A similar post comes up elsewhere in the department.

■ The interviewer recommends you to a colleague in another department.

■ The interviewer recommends you to a contact, friend or ex-colleague who has a relevant job going in another organization.

■ The interviewer leaves to work for another company, where they have to recruit new staff.

People who interview and recruit regularly tend to know about all sorts of jobs other than those they themselves are recruiting for. And if they have no job for you but think you are a talented person, courteous and full of determination, why wouldn't they recommend you to someone else?

# Don't bank on it

As a general rule, it's not worth hanging on forever for a job that may never come up. You may be told you came a close second, and that there may be another job coming up in six months' time. Obviously you need to keep in touch, but keep looking for other work too.

The next job may not happen, or the interviewer may leave the company so you'll end up starting the recruitment process all over again with no guarantee of winning the job at the end of it. Unless you're basically happy where you are, and this is about the only organization you'd want to work for in preference, don't put all your eggs in one basket.

If you want to find yourself a new job, apply for everything that looks interesting and, when you're offered a job you think you'll really enjoy and which offers an increase in prospects or salary or whatever is important to you, take it. In this modern business age, you won't be stuck there forever and there'll be other chances to apply to your dream company – don't hang on indefinitely for a job which may not come up.

And in the meantime, you'll be getting plenty of opportunities to practise what you've learnt. Even when you sense part way through an interview that this isn't the job you want, it's still a perfect opportunity to practise all the skills you've learnt so that when you go for a job you really *do* want, you can be sure you'll give a brilliant interview.

---

**If at first ...**

Don't give up just because you've been turned down for a job. If you're really keen, let the interviewer know it. And keep in touch with them from time to time if you don't find anything else in the interim. Sooner or later, there's every chance it may win you another job. And who knows, it could be even better than the one you originally applied for.

# brilliant CV
second edition
Jim Bright
0273702114
April 2005

*Brilliant CV* is an international bestseller and the UK's bestselling CV book. It remains the only CV book to be based on actual research into what employers and recruiters want to see. Now the fully updated and revised second edition reveals three new chapters and all the latest research. The number one CV guide has just got better!

# brilliant answers
second edition
Susan Hodgson
0273704877
May 2005

What everybody worries about before the interview is what they are going to be asked, and how they should answer it. This bestselling book has been updated and revised and is packed with over 200 of the most commonly asked interview questions - the tricky ones, the hidden meaning ones and the downright tough ones. With one or more ideal answer, to show you exactly what the employer wants you to say - and how to say it.

**Guaranteed to propel you into your dream job!**

**The Brilliant series is the number one job-hunting series, based on actual research into what recruiters are really looking for**

If you wish to find out more about any of these titles or view our full list visit us at:
**www.pearson-books.com**